ISLANDERS

The photograph on the front cover shows two Tory islanders, Dan McClafferty and Willie Diver, returning with the post from Meenlaragh Post Office on the mainland to Tory Island, in Hughie Dixon's half-decker, the *Ave Maria*. Hughie Dixon, a master boat-builder, took eight years to build the *Ave Maria* in the early '50s in his back garden. As there was no electricity on the island then, manual tools had to be used. Hughie was the brother of Jimmy Dixon, the artist who belonged to the Tory Island School of Painting. Over 40 years old, the *Ave Maria* is still in use, though owned on the mainland.

In the background, Errigal Mountain (752 metres) towers above the Donegal hills. This stately cone of white quartzite is the loftiest peak in the county, and the second highest in Ulster. From the summit there is a view extending over six counties, and on a fine day the Scottish islands of Mull and Jura can be seen. This panorama is claimed to be the finest in the entire north of Ireland.

ISLANDERS

The True Story of One Man's Fight to Save a Way of Life

DIARMUID Ó PÉICÍN CI
WITH LIAM NOLAN

Fount
An Imprint of HarperCollins*Publishers*

Fount Paperbacks is an Imprint of
HarperCollins*Religious*
Part of HarperCollins*Publishers*
77–85 Fulham Palace Road, London w6 8jb

First published in Great Britain
in 1997 by Fount Paperbacks

3 5 7 9 10 8 6 4 2

A catalogue record for this book is
available from the British Library

ISBN 0 00 6279988

Printed and bound in Great Britain by
Caledonian International Book Manufacturing Ltd, Glasgow

CONTENTS

Tory Island

Bloody Foreland
Falcarragh
Magheraroarty
Muckish
Mountain
Owey
Iochtar
Gweedore
Aran
Island
Iniscoo
Idirnish
Rutland
Inishkeeragh
Inishfree
Inishal

**COUNTY
DONEGAL**

Tory
Island

Rathlin
Island

**NORTHERN
IRELAND**

Letterkenny
Lifford

Donegal

Inishmurray
Island

Sligo

Inishturbot

EIRE

Galway

Dublin

Inishmore
Inishmaan
Inisheer

**ARAN
ISLANDS**

Blasket
Island

Bear Island
Sherkin Island
Clear Island

THE BECKONING ISLAND

There's a land – oh, it beckons and beckons,
And I want to go back – and I will.
The Spell of the Yukon, Robert W. Service

I'll never forget my first glimpse of Tory Island. It was in June 1980. I'd been exploring the spectacularly beautiful coastline of County Donegal for the first time, and had stopped the car on Bloody Foreland, with its amazing views of the coastline and Muckish Mountain rising over 600 metres in the distance. I turned my gaze from the mainland out across the waters of Tory Sound. Although it was a pleasant day, the sea was quite choppy and the waves were being whipped into white horses by a strong crosswind.

It was then that I saw Tory Island, low and grey, about ten miles away in the distance; a rock about three miles in length, rising from the grip of heavy, rolling seas. It was once described as 'a rock in the middle of the ocean, amongst the birds of the cliffs' (from the nineteenth-century ballad, 'The Herring Song'); although it's not exactly in the middle of the ocean, it's far enough away from the mainland to be one of the most desolate and windswept of all the Irish offshore islands. From where I was standing, I could just about make out the waves breaking against it. It was almost like a great, grey craft newly surfaced from the depths, or a sea monster, immobile on the surface, waiting.

Looking back at that day, I think I knew even then that I was destined to go to Tory Island. What I didn't know, of course, was what the island had in store for me, a 64-year-old Jesuit missionary priest, to all intents and purposes retired, who thought he was in for a quiet life back home in Ireland. So what had drawn me to that desolate spot in the first place?

I was ordained in 1949 by the Archbishop of Dublin, John Charles McQuaid. I began my priestly work as a teacher in various Jesuit schools in Ireland. From there, I travelled to England and with Fr Leonard Shiel, started working as a missionary, beginning at the Liverpool docks. The work suited me, and I was sent all over Britain. I was finally posted much further afield – to Africa. There, in Rhodesia and South Africa, I taught, helped to organize the building of roads and schools and immersed myself in the life and culture of the people. After many years' hard work, my retirement approached. It was the end of my term of office there, and I wanted to spend my last years as a priest in Ireland; I thought I'd earned a quiet spot, and with an increasingly bothersome arthritic hip, returning home seemed the most sensible idea. I also would have the opportunity to do something I had wanted to do for years: learn *Gaeilge* – the Irish language.

All I knew was a *cúpla focail* – a couple of words. That small smattering had stayed with me since my school days. I hated the subject then, mainly because of the way they taught it, and so learnt just enough to scrape through the examinations. However, in the years I spent working in Britain and Africa, the yearning to come to grips with my native tongue grew ever stronger. Once back in Dublin – the city where I was born – and with my retirement years ahead of me, I thought: *Now's* the time to tackle it.

The day after my arrival in Dublin, in September, I began an eight-week course, which turned out to be a difficult ordeal, to say the least! To begin with, I was tongue-tied. I couldn't answer any questions. I found it so frustrating when other pupils seemed to be spouting whole sentences in no time at all, especially when they weren't even Irish like me! At times, I was tempted to quit, like others did, but somehow managed to stick it out to the bitter end. When the two months were up, I knew precious little more Irish than I'd known at the beginning, but was still keen to learn. I soon realized that if I really wanted to learn the language, I'd have to go to a place where it was still spoken; then, if I wanted to communicate with the inhabitants, I'd just have to be able to speak Irish.

So I decided to travel to the Aran Islands (off the west coast of Ireland, beyond Galway Bay) – a *Gaelteacht* (an Irish-speaking area). I arrived on Inishmore (the largest island) in November, and spent a couple of months there. I attended classes at the local school in Eochaill – after all, St Ignatius of Loyola (the founder of the Jesuits) had gone back to school, and what was good enough for him was surely good enough for me! It must have been a peculiar experience for the island children to have an elderly priest among them as a pupil; in fact, they helped me no end. My knowledge of Irish improved considerably, but I still felt I needed more practice. It seemed the natural choice, therefore, when a vacancy for a chaplain in another *Gaelteacht* arose, to volunteer for it. I would be required to say Mass in Irish, and the practice to be gained from that, I reckoned, would do my *Gaeilge* the world of good. The chaplaincy was to a number of Irish-speaking colleges on the Donegal coast, and I was delighted when I found out that I'd been appointed.

So it was that I came to Co. Donegal, and during my explorations found myself driving up along the north-west coast and 'discovering' Tory Island. Maybe it was my experience of island life on Inishmore and my increasing affinity to island people that called me, that fateful June day, to visit Tory Island. Whatever it was, I knew there was a reason I was being drawn there. I drove from Bloody Foreland to the small village of Magheraroarty and went into the local pub to enquire about how one could get out to the island.

'Oh, that's easy enough to arrange, Father,' the landlord told me. 'It's just a matter of keeping an eye out for a boat.' About half an hour later, looking out at the excellent view of the sea from the window, he called to me over his shoulder: 'You're in luck, Father. There's a fishing boat coming in. It's a couple of miles out still, but it won't take long before they're tying up at the pier. You can wander down there then and ask them, make a deal with them.'

I can't remember what the fisherman charged for the return journey, but it wasn't more than a few pounds. Soon we were making our way out into Tory Sound. The waves buffeted the boat; a freshening wind began to sweep away the mist which had initially descended with startling swiftness. I shivered with cold as we neared the island, fastening my coat up tightly, imagining how uncomfortable and hazardous the journey must be in winter.

We went past enormous, almost threatening, cliffs rising about 300 feet from the water, their bases pounded by the crashing waves. Thousands of seabirds caught the wind: cormorants, gulls, puffins. They soared and glided effortlessly on the air eddies, landing in spectacular fashion on precarious ledges. The quality of light, sea-and-sky-influenced, was especially fabulous around the cliffs, where the rocky masses threw deep, purple shadows onto the sea.

From there we passed a long, narrow, steep-sided inlet, which reminded me of a Norwegian fjord. What I could see of the landscape seemed as stark and alien as moonscape, and yet I could hardly wait to step ashore. My curiosity had been awakened, and I knew I had to satisfy it. The half-decker was brought smoothly alongside the pier at Camusmore Bay, roughly at midpoint of the island. I watched, fascinated, as small wavelets, scarcely more than shimmering liquid wrinkles, washed over rounded stones. The half-decker, expertly handled, went in smoothly and gradually came to a stop beside some steps covered in a slippery green algae.

'Mind yourself there, Father, you could lose your footing very easily on that stuff,' called one of the fishermen.

'Thanks,' I said, making my way gingerly up the steps.

I was all set to start exploring the island when I was suddenly approached by a woman, who appeared from out of nowhere. She greeted me in Irish, but I had some difficulty understanding her; her accent, and the Donegal Irish she spoke, sounded very different from the Irish I'd been listening to and trying to learn on Inishmore. There was no mistaking the words *teach sagairt*, 'the priest's house', however. It seemed that, on seeing me in my clericals, she assumed I was on the island for an official visit, and would therefore want to see the local priest. I wasn't, and I didn't. Struggling with the language, I tried to tell her that, in fact, I had come solely to satisfy my curiosity on seeing the island from the mainland. But she started to walk away from the pier and beckoned me to accompany her. It seemed churlish not to follow her, and after a short walk we arrived at the church, St Colmcille's. It was a simple building, with a little burial ground, full of weathered tombstones scattered haphazardly.

The priest, Fr Gallagher, greeted us at the door of his bungalow, next to the church. His eyes lit up when he discovered that I, too, was a priest. He introduced me to the woman who had greeted me at the pier – Rosie Rodgers – and warmly invited me to step inside.

'I won't really, thanks all the same,' I said. 'I just came out to take a look around. I was fascinated by the appearance of the place when I saw it from Bloody Foreland.'

'I know, I know,' he agreed fervently, 'it's marvellous. Look, before you go back in the boat, drop in again for a moment, won't you?'

'All right,' I said, amazed at how pressing he was, how keen he seemed to speak to me. I've often wondered since that day whether what he did could possibly have been done any quicker. I don't think it could.

'Good, good, I'll be expecting you then,' he smiled. '*Maith thú*, good man.'

Because of my visit to *teach sagairt*, the time I had available for a look around the island was severly shortened. I only managed to see a tiny portion of the place: the Tau cross at the head of the slipway; the tower of Colmcille's monastery standing high above the cluster of roofs; the areas of wasteland; the grey and white stone; the pulled-up boats, some of them with their keels in the air, others propped upright to prevent them from toppling over.

All too soon my brief visit was coming to an end, and I made my way back towards the pier. As promised, though, I stopped off to see the priest. What was he so anxious to talk to me about? I soon found out.

'Look, would you like to *come* here?' he asked. 'Sure, you might as well drop in to see the bishop in Letterkenny, have a chat with him.'

I was amazed – he hardly knew me and yet he was already making suggestions about my future! We said goodbye and I hurried to the pier. On the return journey I stood alone up near the bow, looking over the water to Muckish Mountain and Errigal Mountain, Horn Head and the hills of Bloody Foreland on the mainland ahead. We passed a few of the island's boats, fishing inshore.

2

DISPIRITED PEOPLE

I didn't waste any time. I arranged to meet Dr MacFeely, the Bishop of Raphoe, on that very same day. Our chat was brief, yet friendly. I was delighted to see his enthusiasm about my proposal to become the resident curate on Tory Island, and it was especially heartening that he felt it would be an ideal place to learn Irish. He said he would make the requisite arrangements and write to me formalizing the matter. And, indeed, not long after our meeting, I received a letter dated 7 August 1980, which welcomed me to act as the new curate on Tory Island. The priest currently on the island, Fr Gallagher, was to stay until the end of August and I would begin my work from 1 September onwards. I would be paid what were then the normal wages that went with the curacy – £1848 a year.

Dr MacFeely was a frail-looking man, a man who to me seemed tired of life. With hindsight, though, I sometimes wish that I'd pressed him further, that he'd been more forthright and honest about the situation on Tory. It might have saved me much heartache. He knew things he didn't reveal to me. But then, if your health is on the wane and you feel swamped by diocesan problems, the line of least resistance is a powerfully tempting one to take. My more or less unexpected arrival (apparently, after our short meeting, the priest on Tory Island had rung him to suggest I be appointed!) as someone willing to take on a sticky job must have seemed like an answer to a prayer. But I knew nothing of this. Perhaps I should have taken more notice of the curate's attitude, which seemed to be saying loud and strong: 'I just want to get out of this place'; after all, his term of office was not up. But all I had was an instinct that Tory Island was the place for me.

Along with the letter from the Bishop of Raphoe, I received another from Bishop John Murphy, back in Port Elizabeth, South Africa. Murphy was a tremendous character, a man for whom I had great admiration and with whom, I knew, I would get on extremely well. His offer – to return and continue much needed work – was very exciting and attractive, but the offer of Tory was, I knew, what I really wanted. I wrote and thanked Bishop Murphy, saying that much as I would have liked to take up his offer, I felt in conscience that I had to decline. I explained why, hoping he'd understand, and asked him to pray for me. I then formally accepted the position in Tory.

I spent some time in Dublin making various preparations for my trip – for example, having a full medical check-up, because Tory Island didn't have a resident doctor – and taking my leave of old friends. I also tried to find some books about the island's history, which to begin with seemed as if it was going to be a rather fruitless search. I was about to give up, when I came across Robin Fox's *The Tory Islanders – A People of the Celtic Fringe* (Cambridge University Press, 1978), a useful book which contains lots of information about the island's history and development. Fox, an academic, had been a frequent visitor to Tory, and his book carried the dedication '*Do mhuintir an oileáin*': 'to the people of the island'.

Tory Island – *Oilean Thoraigh* – is one of the earliest places mentioned in the bardic history of Ireland. According to the *Ulster Journal of Archaeology* (volume I, 1853), it was 'the stronghold of the Fomorians or African pirates who made many descents on the coast of Ireland at a period so far back in the night of time that it is impossible to bring chronology to bear on it.' The chief mythological figure of those times was Balor of the Evil Eye, the old Celtic god of death, who was supposed to have been God-chief of the pirate race.

Many centuries later, St Colmcille – whose vision and spirituality have transcended the years to the present day – spent time on the island before going on to found his famous community on Iona, off the west coast of Scotland. The remains of Colmcille's tower, over 50 feet tall, still stand in West Town, having withstood the buffeting of gales, rain and sea spray for centuries. It is said that to demonstrate the power of his teachings, and the power that his belief gave to him, Colmcille actually performed a miracle on the island. Using the local clay, believed to have magical powers, he banished all the rats from Tory. The clay is still believed to have the power to ward off disease, prevent seasickness and to keep boats and ships safe while at sea; and there are still no rats on Tory! Of greater significance for my story, legend also has it that Colmcille prophesied that Tory Island would always be inhabited.

Near Colmcille's tower stands the Tau cross (one of two in Ireland, the other being in Kilnaboy, Co. Clare), an ancient Celtic monument standing about six feet high, made from a single block of slate. It is the source of many legends due to some unusual markings on it, including two long, slanted lines. One legendary tale tells that they were caused by the sword of a man (his name is unknown) who hated all religious objects, and who had been given authority to destroy the cross. He was set the task with the peculiar restrictions of having only to use his sword, and only being allowed to strike the cross twice – hence the two lines. Edmund Getty, writing in the *Ulster Journal of Archaeology*, said that 'the confidence of the people in the capability of endurance possessed by this holy emblem was fully warranted by the result, and it retains these proofs of the vain attempt at its destruction.' It seems more likely, however, that the cross is an early example of a St Anthony cross, indicating a link between the early Celtic and Coptic Churches. St John the Baptist's Altar is another ancient monument, which stands near the Tau cross. Getty writes: '... the people belong exclusively to the Roman Catholic Church. A clergyman from Cross-roads, on the opposite coast of Donegall [sic] visits them periodically; or, in a case of urgency, a "curragh" is sent over to bring him. In his absence, prayers are read on Sundays by one of the islanders, at what is called "St John the Baptist's Altar", near the Round Tower.'

A more recent monument stands on the western end of the island – the lighthouse. It was installed in 1832, and rises 90 feet into the air, solid and dramatic in its black and white colouring. In more recent history, Tory was purchased in 1861 (together with some land on the mainland) for a price of £6500 by Benjamin St John Baptist Joule, a businessman from Manchester. He became a classic example of an absentee landlord, who did nothing to help the islanders, yet claimed monies from them. He intended to use force to go and collect the monies if necessary, an option he grew to favour from 1872 onwards, when he didn't receive any rent. The islanders loathed him, understandably angry at the fact that he lived outside Ireland and never visited his land, despite creaming off whatever pathetic few pounds tenants were able to earn in virtual slavery. The islanders would probably have been relieved when the island was finally bought from Joule in 1903 by the Congested Districts Board for Ireland, since it was likely that they'd be treated humanely.

In September 1884 there was a particularly nasty shipwreck off the island; some stories say that it was caused by the so-called King of Tory at that time, Paddy Heggarty, putting a curse on the gunboat (the *Wasp*), which he'd heard was coming to evict the islanders. In fact, an armed force was coming to collect Joule's arrears of £263.15s.8d, sent out from County Mayo on Joule's orders. Admiralty records suggest that the *Wasp* was shipwrecked in Tory Sound because of a 'navigational error', but the legend on Tory suggests otherwise. The story goes that Heggarty summoned the islanders to the cliff top where Tory's cursing stone was buried. He arranged the people in a circle and chanted a spell invoking a curse on the gunboat, actually using the 'cursing stone'. (This was turned from right to left to put a spell on someone who'd done you wrong.) Whatever the effect of the 'cursing stone', the *Wasp* was torn apart on the rocks early one morning, and 50 people were killed. There were six survivors, who were cared for at the lighthouse.

Learning about Tory and its history only made me more eager to begin my journey. Monday 1 September finally arrived, and at 7 a.m. I left Dublin to begin the long drive back to Magheraroarty. I was travelling light – just as in my missionary days – with only a holdall containing Fox's book, a change of clothing, soap, razor, toothbrush and toothpaste and my breviary.

I left for the island around 12.30 p.m., in a boat returning from the mainland. I was filled with a strong sense of anticipation. Looking out once more to Tory, I was reminded of the words I'd been reading in Robin Fox's book, that it was 'an island hovering in elusive mists and filigree-fine rain that clouded it like steam from the cauldron of life itself.' My memory of Tory on that first, brief visit hadn't deceived me. The sight of the cliffs, the sea and the seabirds was just as spellbinding.

I felt buoyed up with the thought of the challenges ahead of me as I walked up to *teach sagairt*. I discovered that it had a small, walled garden of its own; it didn't look like very much grew there, though, probably because it was too close to the shore and would get drenched by wind-blown salty spray. I was standing by the wall of the garden, when a woman emerged from a nearby house, holding the front of her cardigan closed against the wind. She greeted me, saying, '*Dia dhuit, a Athair. Fáilte rómhat*': 'Hello, Father, welcome.' She had a key in her hand, told me her name was Kathleen, and opened the door of the house, pushing it in for me to enter. She asked me why I had come to the island, and I told her that I wanted to learn Irish. She made no comment, so I took the key from her outstretched hand and thanked her. When I turned to close the door behind me, I saw children, women and men coming inquisitively out of the houses to see what was going on. The woman spoke to them in Irish, and whatever it was she said, they looked surprised.

I was just as surprised when I discovered that the curate had already gone! It appeared he had actually left at the end of July, leaving the islanders without priest or Mass for the entire month of August. He left no note, nor instructions of any kind. It didn't feel quite right, somehow.

I didn't think too much more about it during that first week, though. The house was comfortable enough inside, and there was plenty of turf to ensure warm fires. I gradually began to get to know the island and find out more about its people. I visited the places I'd read about in my book, touching the cold stones of Colmcille's tower and the Tau cross; it felt as if I was putting my fingers onto direct links with events and people of earlier centuries.

I got to know the path between West Town – which comprised two rows of houses facing one another, including my house (and the church) and the Post Office – and East Town, the only other settlement on the island, with its cluster of 24 houses and its small harbour, Port Doon. The entire population can't have been more than 200.

My arrival had obviously caused some excitement. During those first few days exploring I noticed many people watching me from their houses. It is impossible to arrive on Tory without being observed. The inhabitants are always on the look out for the arrival of *strainséiri* – strangers, or for their own coming back from the mainland, or the men coming home from the sea. When I did see them in the street they put their heads down and passed by; if they did look up it was with a mixture of inquisitiveness and suspicion.

I also began to notice some other things which puzzled and worried me. A huge pile of rubbish lay and was spreading near the top of the pier. It turned out that there was no rubbish collection, so people just dumped their rubbish where others dumped theirs. The road between West Town and East Town was pitted, rutted and pot-holed. It was in a frightful state of disrepair, but nothing was being done about it. I noticed that many houses were boarded up and derelict. I then discovered that there was no sewage system, no piped water, no fuel (the island's turf resources had been depleted many years ago), and the only transportation links they had with the mainland were the fishing boats. The pier and slipway at West Town had obviously been constructed many years before, and were inadequate given the severe storms which I knew the island experienced. The island's only generator had been allowed to deteriorate to such a state that about one hour's electricity a day was as much as the islanders could get.

I didn't understand it. Why had the island been allowed to deteriorate like this? My time on Inishmore had taught me that island life *was* hard, that it was a struggle and yet the people had a hardy individuality about them which meant they coped. Here on Tory, a bald island on which not a single tree grew, an island that was literally a shelf of rock in the ocean, it was obvious that people must have *wanted* to stay and therefore would have expected to experience struggle and hardship just to survive, and yet the inhabitants I saw didn't seem to be determined to survive, no matter what that struggle would entail. Their faces, and their very demeanour, suggested nothing but an air of demoralization. The community I had come to looked broken and hurt, not tough and hardy. I knew that something wasn't right. Why weren't the islanders working for their island? Why were they so dispirited? *What had I got myself into?*

I knew that to find out what was happening I had to get to know the people well, to talk to them, but it seemed an impossible task; for many, I was just the replacement priest who had come to fill the gap left by the man who had left them Mass-less in August. My reason for coming to the island didn't seem to have been believed, and if that were so, what did it say about their relationship with my predecessor?

So I went out and about, knocking on doors, meeting people, talking to them. People like Pádraig Mac Rúairí. Pádraig was one of those islanders who had 'come home'; in his case, it meant leaving London and returning to the spot which kept on calling him. This *dúchais* – a pull or call – was a feeling that many people experience, I was to find out. People like Pádraig Óg Rodgers, the island's hereditary *Árd Rí* – High King. (This was an island tradition; a 'King' was elected by the people when an occasion required more than usual deliberation, someone to make the final decision.) I met Shane Rogers, the island's Peace Commissioner. A brother of Pádraig Mac Rúairí, he was married to Maureen, and they had two children, Micheál and Ann Marie. Together, they ran a little general store in West Town. Then there was resourceful, imaginative Féilimidh Doohan, who lived near the pier and could turn his hand to anything, including making wheelbarrows! And Paddy Boyle, a fisherman whose wife Nábla was such a talented actress and singer. I soon discovered that there were some marvellous characters here, people I knew I was going to get on with. I was pleased that I'd made the effort to get out and meet them; I was sure that any suspicions they had about me would gradually lessen if they got to know me well too.

Over the next few weeks I was to learn much about the hardships of island life. The islanders had it tough – unemployment was almost total. Certainly, in fine weather some fishing was done, but it was a diminishing and dying way of earning a living. The fishermen's crafts were too small to venture out on extended trips into the deeper Atlantic where fish abounded, so they were confined to what was virtually part-time inshore fishing where the pickings were meagre. On top of that, they could only fish when their boats could be safely launched. Weather changes were swift and violent, and getting the boats out of the water and far enough up the shore to escape the thundering wind-driven waves took strength, speed, patience and team-work. They had no harbour or sheltered anchorage; the boats had to be kept out of the water during the autumn and winter months because the storms could make matchwood of a boat in minutes. Their lives came to resemble repeated exercises in futility and endurance.

The half-deckers – long, wide-beamed, heavy, clinker-built and with weighty engines close to the stern – took a lot of careful manoeuvring and man-handling, even when hitched up to a straining tractor. It was nothing unusual to see a crowd of as many as 15 or 20 men and boys, and occasionally women and girls as well, labouring to get a half-decker positioned for the haul up the slip. It was serious, sweat-inducing work, and no sooner would one boat be chocked up and secured than the group would immediately start on the task of getting another safely ashore, the urgency of the task driving everyone to all-out efforts to save their boats from the merciless elements. This also affected the other main sea-based occupation, that of collecting seaweed for making iodine-rich kelp.

As for farming, only a third of the whole surface of Tory could be used for arable farming – and then even barely so. Scrubland, rock and bog predominated. Crops could not be ensured from year to year. There was, therefore, a sort of inevitability to the downward spiral of spirits which took hold of the islanders. Merely staying alive seemed to be the name of the game. They never seemed to have much to look forward to; indeed some admitted to me that sometimes there was no real reason to get out of bed in the mornings.

Added to these bitter tales were rumours, snippets of information here and there – they didn't fully make sense to me, but went some way to explaining their attitude and the state of the island. People would talk of leaving, one day saying 'we're going', the next 'we're not going' and then 'we'll wait and see' – but why? Why leave this beautiful, captivating island? When I asked why the island was in such a ruinous state, I was told, 'Oh, it's *them*, Father, they just don't care.' Who were *they*?

My feelings of unease grew even stronger when I met one of the lighthouse keepers. They were the only people living on the island who found the journey to and from the mainland easy – they were ferried by helicopter. I'd gone out to the lighthouse, on the western shores of the island, and looked down over the cliffs to the sea, imagining what the scene must have been like on the morning of the shipwreck of the *Wasp*. Even with a fresh, westerly breeze blowing and the sounds of the seas lashing the rocks, there *must* have been human cries and screams mingled in with the rending of iron and brass and timber, and the rifle-crack noise of wind-whipped canvas sails ripping apart. I wondered whether Heggarty had *really* assembled a group of islanders there to invoke a curse on the gunboat. I began to realize that fiction and fact, superstition and mythology were very much entwined in the mindset of the Tory islanders. It made trying to ascertain what was happening much more difficult.

It was then that I bumped into one of the keepers, who immediately asked me, 'Do you know where you *are*, Father?'

I must have looked puzzled, because he said, 'You know you're on broken bottles here?'

I truly didn't know what he was talking about. I tried to get more out of him, but he wouldn't explain any further.

During those first six days on the island, I was gradually becoming aware of something awful, something sinister at work. I was at an utter loss to know what it was. I must have spent six sleepless nights worrying about the islanders, wondering whether I'd done the right thing in coming, debating whether I should just leave and praying to God to help me choose the right path.

It seemed no time at all until I had to start preparing for my first Mass on the island. How would I fare, I wondered. Apart from the fact that the church was freezing, and always had an air of dampness in it – even on good days – what would they think of me? I'd be able to get through the liturgy in Irish, I'd learnt it carefully, but my accent was different to theirs – would they be able to understand me?

Virtually the entire island population was in the church when I walked out on to the altar at 11 a.m. Over half of them were from

West Town; the others had walked along the rutted, narrow road from East Town. The only ones who didn't come to Mass were the very old or those too ill to attend. I was too occupied by the celebration of the Mass itself (and, of course, the effort to concentrate on reading the Irish correctly) to focus properly on faces and expressions. But I could sense that things weren't right. It was a kind of oppressive silence, even though people were in close proximity. The lighthouse keeper's question haunted me: 'Do you know where you *are*, Father?' After that first Mass I decided I had to find out once and for all what was happening.

It was Jimmy Duggan who pointed me in the right direction. Jimmy was a fisherman by trade. An accomplished singer and traditional dancer – I would later discover! – he was sturdily built, with high cheekbones and straight hair. He was also rather shy, to begin with. I soon got to know his wife, Gráinne, as well – a marvellous woman. Jimmy had the task of going to every house on the island taking note of the meter readings for electricity consumption – not that there was much electricity to consume.

He was also the secretary of the island's declining co-operative. This non-profit-making organization was one of many that sprang up all over Ireland. One of the founder members of the Co-operative movement was another Jesuit, Fr Thomas Finlay. The idea behind the movement was to build up communities through them, but sadly they were not conspicuously successful. The co-operative on Tory was founded in 1969, one of its main aims being to get electricity for the island. By the time I arrived, the co-operative had weakened and was virtually non-existent; in fact, Jimmy and his notebook were the only relics of it.

'Go and talk to the County Council,' he said. 'Go and ask them about their plans for the island. Ask their friend, the one that always pushes the Council line. They go ahead and make up their minds and do something, or refuse to do something, and we're powerless to complain or make our feelings known. They don't give a damn about us.'

'But what *is* going on?' I replied anxiously. 'Why won't people tell me what's happening?'

Maybe it was because I was a stranger. I wasn't one of them, I hadn't been born on the island. I felt they accepted me but I didn't know how far they trusted me.

I was soon to find out the truth.

I'd never had any dealings with politicians of any party – as far as I was concerned it was all uncharted seas. I hadn't had any truck with bishops either, other than on the day I was ordained, social occasions during my time in Africa and my meeting with Bishop MacFeely before I came to Tory. I'd never really been a rebellious priest, but here I was, about to try to 'take on' someone in authority. I didn't even know where the County Council offices were!

Jimmy told me they were in Lifford, so I soon made the necessary arrangements to cross to the mainland in a half-decker and collect my car from where I had parked it at Magheraroarty. I consulted a road map, found that Lifford was about 45 miles away inland, cheek-by-jowl with the town of Strabane, Northern Ireland, and set off along the roads of Co. Donegal.

I eventually arrived at the County Council offices, explained who I was, and asked to talk to someone about Tory Island and the plans, if any, the Council were making for it. I was referred to one official after another, each professing to know nothing about it. As I was passed from one official to another, my patience wore thinner. I had come all the way from the island, I'd driven right across the county thinking, naively, that I would get some answers. When I couldn't take any more, I snapped.

'I want to see your file on Tory Island,' I demanded of the representative from the Housing Department. 'I want to know what the official situation is regarding the island.'

He started to make excuses, but I held up my hand and said, 'Now wait a minute, hear me out. There's something very odd going on that I must get to the bottom of. Who's in charge? I need to speak to whoever is in charge. I want information. I want it now!'

'*Please!*' he said. 'It stinks – stinks to high heaven!'

'What does? What are you talking about?'

'Tory,' he finally answered. 'Father, if I were you, I'd forget about it. Honestly. Just let it drop.'

There was a finality about the manner in which he turned away and busied himself with some papers. I stood there for a minute or two. Clearly something awkward, something hidden, was being kept under official wraps. But what? Had I touched a raw nerve? He refused to answer any more of my questions. Where to turn to now? How was I going to breach the wall of official silence and get the information I required? Back on the island, it came to me – journalists.

I contacted a reporter on the local newspaper, the *Donegal Democrat*, and explained the situation – who I was, the troubling conditions and distraught people I had landed amongst, and my experience at the County Council offices.

'There might be a story in this for you,' I said. 'I'm wondering if you'd help me find out what's going on. There must be some official records, minutes, reports or *something*. Might you be in a position to dig something up?'

He expressed interest, said he'd look into it and would get back to me if he found anything out. The very next day he rang back and said, 'Are you sitting down? Have you a glass of water handy? You might need it!'

'Is it as bad as that?' I asked.

'I'll leave you to decide,' he said grimly. 'Now, where to start?'

I listened in horror to what he had to say – he had been told that the County Council had carried out a survey of those inhabited offshore islands which came within its jurisdiction; that a secret report prepared in 1978 had recommended that the islands be evacuated and shut down; that the County Council had decided to implement the recommendation. Further, he said he had been informed that the Council viewed Tory Island as being suitable for only three uses: as a firing range, for quarantine purposes, or for the siting of a high security prison.

Conscientious journalist that he was, he was not prepared to divulge to me the source of his information. If it was accurate (and I believed, still believe, it was), it explained much: the neglect of essential services such as roads and generators, the failure to invest in and develop the island, and the making available, instead, of Council housing on the mainland. (Apparently, £650,000 had already been set aside by the Council for the construction of housing at Falcarragh – a particularly cruel decision since not a single new house had been built on Tory in the previous 50 years.) If the information *wasn't* accurate, it made even worse the way the Council had been dealing with Tory Island and its inhabitants.

I couldn't believe it. The Council, supposedly a caring public body whose resources should have been used to help the common good, were apparently determined to destroy one of the most independent-minded living *Gaelteachts* in the country, along with its ancient folklore and tradition. How could the living culture of Tory simply be shut down? Running through all communities is the obligation, the necessity, to preserve native cultures and tradition. Language is one of the principal channels through which culture and tradition are both learned and preserved, and passed on from one generation to another, one era to another. The Irish language has a history extending back over a thousand years, and extant literature in the Irish language predates that of any living European language other than Greek. Pope John Paul II himself, on his visit to Ireland in September 1979, spoke Irish: '*Moladh go deó le Dia*' – 'May God be praised for ever'; thus saluting the rich tradition that enshrined the faith of the country. Language preserves a way of life, and on Tory, the real Irish way of life was more alive than in any other *Gaelteacht* area. The age-old customs were still cherished, the ancient sayings were still known to the people and still used in their conversations. For this reason alone, I felt, for anyone even to contemplate uprooting the Irish-speaking community of Tory Island, with its indissoluble links to the ancient past, was monstrous.

The outrage which flooded through me at the situation I'd uncovered increased in intensity. I'd fight the injustice, and I'd help the islanders to fight as well. It was entirely predictable that the County Councillors would deny my accusations. Tory was bleak, remote and inaccessible, yes, but that was no excuse for the employment of injustice against its people, the inheritors of an ancient tradition.

3

'WE'LL FIGHT UNTIL WE DROP!'

I knew instinctively that there was precious little time to wallow in theories as to how to proceed. We had to be practical. Something had to be done for and by the islanders now to save their homes, their culture and their heritage. I couldn't stand idly by merely observing the Council's continuing dereliction of its responsibilities towards the island. I decided to try to halt the shameful process.

There had been other island evacuations, which had been desperately fought against. For example, that of Inishturbot Island, one of the most complete early Christian monastic settlements in Europe and the subject of the BBC/RTE documentary 'An Island Here, An Island There'. In November 1948, Inishmurray Island (off the coast of Co. Sligo) was evacuated. Patrick Heraughty, a doctor who spent the first 12 years of his life on Inishmurray, wrote that 'it was with great reluctance that the islanders agreed to it; the older people especially deeply regretted it in later years' (*Inishmurray*, The O'Brien Press, Dublin, 1982). 'Later years' was too late – by then the island was *marbh*, dead. Inishmurray became an officially designated bird sanctuary.

In 1953 the controversial evacuation of Blasket Island (off the south-west Kerry coast) took place. The inhabitants were frequently storm-bound for weeks at a time, and like Tory lacked many essential services. Yet they fought hard to stay on their island; sadly, all of them had to leave, the last being taken off in late November of that year. How could I possibly sit back and allow another event like these be re-enacted on Tory? Tory has, if anything, a very long memory – surely the islanders would know of the savage massacre of 1608, where the fugitives of Sir Cahir O'-Doherty were killed by Sir Arthur Chichester's army? Surely they wouldn't want to become the victims of another senseless battle?

I hurried around the island, talking to people and finding out exactly what they had been told. All was confusion, with people hearing rumour after rumour. No one was exactly sure what was happening, no one was keeping them informed of the situation.

All they *did* know was pressure, persuasion, even veiled threats, to leave the island and take up new accommodation on the mainland. It turned out that some had already left; I was gradually to hear about the ensuing drink and marital problems that many began to face once they'd left their homes.

Everyone I spoke to was passionate about the island, many spoke with tears in their eyes as they described their feelings at the thought of leaving. Tory was their home, it was where they wanted to remain. Time and time again I heard the phrases 'We have every right to stay here' and 'No matter where you are, the place where you were born and reared is the place you love'. As Pádraig Mac Rúairí told me, 'See him?' – he pointed to his son – 'This is where I want him to be, here on Tory. It's where I want *us* to be.' There was no way that Jimmy Duggan would leave either. He was determined to preserve the ancient culture and traditions, a fierce and gifted custodian of the old ways.

And who was doing anything to try to help the islanders? No one. The barred windows and barred doors of the island's empty houses were symbols of the effects of official neglect. The living conditions on the island were unmistakably terrible. Those faceless bureaucrats, possessed of responsibility without accountability, had deliberately let basic facilities run down over the years. The islanders of Tory had no running water, no refuse collection, no sewage system. The island's only road was left to deteriorate into crumbling disrepair. The electricity supply was disgracefully inadequate and dwindling. There was no resident doctor, no dentist, no harbour or breakwater; access to and from the island was totally inadequate and hazardous. The population had plummeted from 400 (approximately a century ago) to 200. People were uncertain, depressed and suspicious; their spirit was so low they found it hard to look you straight in the eye. They were dangerously close to total demoralization.

More importantly, perhaps, why was the Church not openly condemning the Council? Why was it remaining silent and passive, when by my reckoning it should have been active in fighting for the islanders' rights? No official statements were made. No open support was forthcoming.

It was clear that the islanders weren't helping themselves. They'd given up the struggle. Pádraig Mac Rúairí was a good case in point. Pádraig hadn't had it easy, mind. Several years suffering from depression and alcohol-related problems had put an enormous strain on his marriage. Sometimes he couldn't even face getting out of bed, let alone venturing out of the house. Talking to him about the future of the island, I began to learn more about the state of their lives.

'You don't understand the situation, Father,' he'd say. 'On this island if you haven't got a boat, and you've got no turf, and you've got no food … I haven't even got a proper house to live in. *Look* at it! Is it any wonder I don't get out of bed sometimes?'

It was attitudes like his that I knew I had to try to change. For a start, I had to get them motivated, get them to believe in themselves and get them to realize that things *could* be done. They didn't *have* to go under, didn't *have* to succumb, didn't *have* to sink further into a state of demoralization and helplessness just because mainland-based bureaucrats had decided that they should leave their island homes. I wanted them to reach a stage where they would stand up for themselves, speak up for themselves, and say to one another 'Look, *this* is the way we should be tackling this.'

A plan of campaign was needed if we were going to win. There were many practical problems on the island that we had to face and solve. We needed to raise publicity about the island, we needed to work together and fight for our rights.

I also knew that I had to tread carefully. I now realized that the initial wariness with which I was treated by the islanders was a result of their previous relations with those in authority, and the fear that I was going to take the side of the local authorities.

'Sometimes the priests we had on the island were very good to us,' I was told by one man, 'but a lot of them were the opposite. Don't take *my* word alone.'

Their attitude, initially, was one of '*Ná bí beag ná mór leis*' – in essence, don't be too friendly with him, but don't ignore him either. I had to get them to see that I was on their side, that I would fight for their basic human rights as long as it was necessary. We were racing into winter with its storms and isolation. It would be a time of hurricane force gales, numbing cold, stinging rain and spray, rough seas, boats and ships blown off course, and the island and its people taking hammering after hammering. I knew that it was going to be an immensely difficult task that lay ahead of us, and realized that I would have to be as strong as possible for them.

So what made me think that I could somehow lead them in all of this? Where did my fighting spirit come from? I don't know. Does anyone know precisely why he or she is tough, or cynical, or artistic, or gentle, or gullible – or whatever? I don't think so. We are what we are. Though experiences and circumstances may tend to shape us, it is whatever character we are born with, allied to whatever faith we grow up with, that ultimately determines how we behave. I'd like to think – in fact, I *know* – that my determination to lead the islanders stemmed from my priesthood.

I've always known that I was called to the priesthood. I've never wanted to do anything else. A priest is there for his people; when you hear the people of a parish saying 'The priest is behind us', you know you're hearing about a priest who is really doing his job. I often imagine what it must have been like in the very early days of Christianity. Although there were immense hardships to face, there was enough strength and inspiration for the Christians to spread the Word of God. As a Jesuit, it is also my primary role to preach, teach and catechize.

Moreover, I couldn't ignore the pledge that I had made to my Order, in the light of its Fourth Decree made at the thirty-second General Congregation in 1974–1975, that 'the mission of the Society of Jesus today is the service of faith, of which the promotion of justice is an absolute requirement.' I would use the 'Discernment of Spirits' to help me in my duty. This is a sort of checklist of behaviour, a kind of spiritual DIY manual centred on the task of trying to distinguish whether an idea or impulse in the soul comes from the good spirit or the evil spirit. A distinguished fellow Jesuit, John A. Hardon, wrote:

> *In persons who are seriously intent on doing God's will, the good spirit is recognized by the peace of mind and readiness for sacrifice that a given thought or desire produces in the soul.*

My peace of mind was often tenuous, and often wavered alarmingly, but I was ready for sacrifice. I was empowered to go on because I knew the validity of the actions I had to take. The words of Fr Tim Hamilton's unpublished 1987 report on 'The Priest and Social Action', say it all:

> The need for social action ... is extreme and growing ... The effects of poverty, unemployment, bad housing, poor education and poor health are being felt increasingly, especially as the necessary resources to meet these needs are being more and more restricted. A particular need is felt by neglected minorities, especially in remote areas ... since Vatican II, the Church's role in social action has been seen as being more central in the process of evangelization ... the promotion of justice is an integral part of the mission of the Gospel.

Pope John Paul II, preaching to the bishops of Latin America in 1979 said:

> The Church feels the duty to proclaim the liberation of millions of human beings; the duty to help this liberation becomes firmly established.

On Tory Island I identified totally with the words of the Holy Father. I had been thrown into the heart of a human crisis, and had to use my abilities and experience to do the best I could – with the grace of God, of course. I simply bore in mind the Church's teaching that all persons are created in the image of God – *imago Dei*; its simple, yet profound, truth became the underlying factor in my struggle.

If there's one thing in my life that will always help me face any struggle ahead, it's the way I tackle problems. I like to think that I live in the real world, not a world of theological abstractions. As a result, I always elect to go for straightforward action, rather than become swamped by agonized theorizing. And I'm not afraid to stand up for what I believe in either, as this incident from my seminary days shows.

We weren't allowed to smoke, and I thought it was daft. I felt hemmed in and ruled by an unnecessary amount of behavioural restrictions, so much so that one day I said to a group of my friends, 'Surely to God we could be allowed to have a cigarette. I'm going to go and see the Superior and ask him.'

They didn't think I'd have the nerve, but I didn't think it was any big deal. The Superior listened without interruption and when I finished he asked, 'Can you give me any reason why I should allow you to smoke?'

'Because I'd *like* to smoke,' I said.

Whether it was because I had the guts to stick my neck out, I don't know, but he granted me permission to smoke. When I went back to where my companions were waiting someone asked, 'Well?'

I maintained a serious, downcast expression for a few moments until I could hold it no longer, then said gleefully, 'Well, fellas, today I'm going to smoke!'

I didn't particularly enjoy smoking that much, but, you see, even at that stage I couldn't see any sense in lying down unquestioningly in the face of rules or regulations that I didn't agree with.

My first task was to get the islanders behind me, to get them ready and willing to fight. So I began to use the few minutes at the end of Mass every Sunday as a valuable opportunity to rally them to the cause.

'You can lie down and capitulate in the face of the treatment you're getting,' I told them, 'or we can all roll up our sleeves and get some work done. You don't have to accept what's being dished out to you. You have rights. But you need to get your spirits up, and you need to get back your human dignity and your self-belief. As islanders, you're not marginals, or people living outside of society, you've always been inside – inside the structure which made you "beings for others". The solution here isn't to integrate you into the structure of mainland culture, but to transform the island itself, so that you actually become "beings for yourselves". '

The islanders had to believe they had a future. I assured them of that, and assured them of my help. I told them: 'We'll fight until we drop!'

4

THE START OF THE BATTLE

How I wished we had the kind of money the County Council had laid aside for building new houses in Falcarragh! As it was, we had hardly anything. But I knew that we had to get on anyway and deal with our money problems later. I'd do anything possible to get what we needed. I knew, though, that any initiatives had to involve the islanders fully. In that way, their self-confidence and self-belief would increase, and their desire to fight for their homes would strengthen.

In October 1980, the first job I got the islanders to tackle was the road between West Town and East Town. It was Jimmy Duggan who prompted me when he said, 'The road is in a terrible condition. It's full of potholes and the surface is crumbling away. Maybe doing something about it would be a good start.'

We held a public meeting in the school, and the following Sunday I announced from the altar that road repairs would be the work for the week, and for every week until it was completed. About ten men volunteered their services. Some of them had spent short periods off the island, working as labourers in Scottish or

English cities, but couldn't really be classified as experienced road builders. But their attitude was what mattered – they were willing, happy to co-operate and proud. The only experience I had of road construction was from my time in Africa, but that was purely with the mobilization of small work forces to get the job done – I knew nothing at all about road-repair techniques. I wasn't exactly in Samson's class when it came to strength and fitness either, so I didn't think I'd be able to help as much as I wanted to.

'That doesn't matter at all, Father,' they said. 'You can be the ganger!'

We decided to start the job at East Town. Luckily, there were some broken stones left over from whenever the road had last been repaired, but one essential ingredient was missing – tar. Unfortunately, there wasn't anything we could do about it; dry stones and gravel, however hard the mixture was pounded into the potholes, would undoubtedly be sluiced out again by rain and wind when the weather turned sour. We just had to do what we could.

The ditch-like channel that ran beside the road had become choked and overgrown over the years, and also needed to be cleared. It was rough, tough, physical work, and they went about it with a great willingness and expenditure of effort. They were a revelation as well as an inspiration. I knew full well that any or all of them would be perfectly entitled to thumb their noses at me and tell me to leave. But no one did. It was as if they realized, both figuratively and factually, that this could possibly be their last ditch.

They didn't let me remain ganger for very long. It was put to me diplomatically that they didn't need my presence with them every day, and that they were perfectly willing and capable of working unsupervised. I was delighted to see their commitment, but felt a little sad I hadn't helped them as much as I should.

However, I suppose it gave me time to get going on other projects for the island. I didn't go and check on their progress continually, either. I just contented myself by asking occasionally, 'Well, how's the work going, men?'

They assured me that it was 'going great' and that they'd tell me when it was ready. I could hardly believe the day when Jimmy came to the house and said, 'Father, you can come along now and see what we've done.'

Not only had they repaired the road between the two villages, but they'd also built a new road leading down to the houses. I really felt that this wonderful achievement was a fresh start for them, for all of us; their accomplishment was a great beginning.

It wasn't long after the road was finished that I was visited at *teach sagairt* by a serious-faced deputation consisting of Jimmy Duggan and Paddy Boyle.

'Father,' Jimmy began, 'we have a problem.'

'Go on,' I encouraged him, curious as to what I would hear.

'You see, it's the electricity,' he continued.

I looked up at the light, which happened to be switched on. There was no lack of electricity in the priest's house – it had its own generator. What was the problem for them?

'Father,' Paddy said, 'we have to buy diesel for the generator, but we've no money, and we've no diesel.'

'Well, how much would the right amount of diesel cost?' I asked.

'About £600,' answered Paddy quietly.

I stared in disbelief. Not only had the amount of electricity available to the islanders dwindled to a trickle, now they were facing a total stop, with no way forward. What on earth would they do without electricity? My mind had gone a total blank as to what I should suggest, but I couldn't convey that to them.

'Gentlemen,' I said, sounding far more confident than I felt, 'leave it to me.'

The look of relief which immediately spread over their faces was wondrous to behold, but I quickly ushered them out of the house in case they should detect my rising panic.

'Lord,' I prayed, 'if this is the way it's got to be, I trust you, but I need your help, I can't do it alone. Help me to remember the promise that neither I, nor anyone else, will be tested beyond what we can bear.' A line from Psalm 55 came to mind: 'Cast your burden on the Lord, and He will sustain you'.

'Sustain *me*, Lord,' I added.

After much deliberation, I picked up the phone and rang the Allied Irish Bank branch office at Falcarragh. I asked to be put through to the manager; when he eventually came on the line I told him who I was, where I was phoning from, and that I needed a loan to cover the purchase of diesel for the generator on Tory Island. Silence. I held my breath – was he going to ask me whether I was crazy, didn't I know that no loans were ever given to Tory islanders?

Then he replied, 'Father, how much are you looking for?'

'About £600?' I replied tentatively. 'And I can personally guarantee that figure.'

Fingers crossed. Silence.

'That'll be fine, Father, no problem,' he finally said.

I clenched my fist in triumph. I'd done it!

'Thank you very much,' I said warmly. Oh, and thank you, Lord, I added with a smile. As a result, the loan was granted and the facility given. The diesel oil was sent out to the island.

So we'd made a start. There was no overnight miracle change in the islanders' demeanour, but they gradually began to hold their heads up and start thinking about what they could do to help themselves. Not that this was so easy, when there was still a sense of dereliction, with so many houses barred up and abandoned.

One person who I was delighted to see get to work was Pádraig Mac Rúiarí. I'd challenged him to start repairing his house; I knew he could do it, if only he were encouraged. If I could get him a grant, or part of a grant, would he begin work on a chimney and fireplace? Thankfully, he agreed, and I set about getting the much-needed resources. I obtained a grant of about £500 for house improvements from *Roinn Na Gaelteachta*. (This was the government department with the greatest influence over decision-making relating to Tory Island. Based in Dublin, it had responsibility for *all* the Irish-speaking communities. It had no particular ties to the Donegal County Council, any more than it had with, say, the Galway County Council.) As well as the grant for Pádraig, grants would eventually be given for the construction of two chalets, public toilets and a community hall!

It was actually while I was watching how his construction work was progressing that I witnessed at first hand how the Council was trying to persuade people to evacuate their homes and leave for the mainland. One islander was acting – albeit unofficially – on the Council's behalf. He was a facilitator, persuader, if you like. A big, gruff man, he came in unannounced.

'My God,' he said, 'what a dump! You haven't even got a chimney!'

Pádraig continued working, explaining that he was actually building one himself.

'Are you not putting your name down for a house on the mainland?' persisted the man.

'No, I'm not,' Pádraig answered firmly.

'You've only got a day or two left to make up your mind,' the man said. 'Your neighbours have their names down. You'll be left out. You'll be left here when they're all gone. Suit yourself. Don't say I didn't warn you.'

He turned and walked out, calling 'What a dump!' over his shoulder.

Pádraig was humiliated and embarrassed, and I tried hard to reassure him.

'Take no notice,' I said. 'Put him out of your mind.'

'How can I not take notice, Father? *You* heard him.'

I was painfully aware that this type of scene – the same threatening behaviour, the same vulnerability searched out and exploited – was still taking place in houses all over the island, even while we had begun to work together and fight the possibility of evacuation. Some families, sadly, did succumb to the treatment and put their names on the list.

The longer my stay on Tory, the more I was compelled to keep on fighting, encouraging the islanders and working with them for survival. Not that it wasn't hard, mind. Especially at that early stage, I went through periods of personal doubt. I didn't know if I was strong enough to endure what I knew would be a hard struggle. I repeatedly asked myself whether what I was doing, what we were attempting to do, was the right course of action in the circumstances. My nights were often punctuated by sleeplessness, and in that twilight zone between wakefulness and fitful dozing, I'd struggle with the question: God, what am I doing in this place? I knew I had the option of leaving, of saying that I felt too old for such rigours as had awaited me. Should I leave?

What with all the work taking place, I took to going on long walks by myself whenever I needed to clear my mind. I was increasingly feeling like a mouse on a treadmill and there wasn't a lot of time to stand and admire my surroundings. But when I forced myself to do it, and the conditions were right, I would feel an interior sense of wonder. I'd watch a lone half-decker anchored off the cliffs, or edging carefully towards the rocks where the lobster pots lay on the sea floor, and wonder whether the fishermen were as consciously affected by their surroundings as I was. When I saw the physical evidence of God's power on the island – the wind and sea sculpting the rocks and the bay – it only made me more determined to fight on. Why had the community been isolated, why were their rights being ignored? The word 'pariah' may not be amongst the most common in their lexicon, but the islanders understood its meaning well enough.

I felt so angry every time I thought about the officials back on the mainland, hiding behind their impenetrable bureaucratic smokescreen. The words of Brook Atkinson (*Once Around The Sun*, Harcourt Brace & Co, 1951) very accurately reflect the treatment meted out to the islanders; indeed, they reflect the treatment I was to encounter when I began to fight on their behalf: 'Bureaucracies are designed to perform public business. But as soon as a bureaucracy is established, it develops an autonomous spiritual life, *and comes to regard the public as its enemy*' (my italics).

To quote the journalist Fintan O'Toole (writing in the *Irish Times* in a different context), the mentality which resulted in Tory's people being treated as they were

is one in which society is understood as a set of abstract, atomized individuals rather than as a community of mutual responsibility. It is one in which individuals are seen to have legal rights rather than human rights, perceived as claimants rather than citizens ... The answer lies not just in individual failures, but in a whole set of ideas and attitudes. The culture of individualism in which people are seen as legal entities rather than as members of a community is part of that set. So, too, is the idea that the State itself is somehow distinct from the people ... The gap between the State and the people is the problem we have. It is a gap between law and justice, between bureaucracy and democracy, between the State as an expression of a human community, and the State as a denial of that community.

A community is a group of people who share effective bonds and a culture, a set of values, a common history and identity, a purpose and an ability to act in unison. Confronted with a community of victims (for that was what the Tory islanders had become) I had no alternative but to stick by them. They felt they didn't have a voice – I'd be their voice until they found their own. They felt they were powerless against the bureaucrats – I'd try to disprove that. They thought a move to the mainland was inevitable – we'd have something to say about that. But the fight against bureaucrats wasn't going to end that year, or the next, or the next. It's going on even now, all these years later.

Sadly, as uncomfortable and unpalatable as it is for me to say this, I suffered as much from Church bureaucracy as I did from the lay or governmental kind. If you re-read the words of Fintan O'Toole, substituting the word 'Church' for 'State', I think that a pretty accurate picture can be glimpsed of the role played by some members of the Catholic Church in Ireland. They let down the people of Tory Island. The failure of the Church authorities to stand up for the rights of the islanders was shameful and scandalous. There had been no public expression of solidarity with the islanders. Instead, there had been a timidity on the part of the Church in its dealings with the State and matters relating to Tory. What had my predecessors on Tory Island been like? What marks had Tory left on them, and they on it? I heard rumours that some priests had co-operated with the local government in helping to encourage the islanders to move, but it was something I didn't want to believe. If their timidity had become so diluted that it had degenerated into collusion, the scandal was all the greater. I'd heard, more than once, that Tory Island was a place where priests were sent to dry out or to straighten out. But I wasn't someone who needed a cure from either of those conditions.

If they thought I'd settle in quietly while Tory was gradually stripped of its life, then they were wrong.

I feel that it's all part of the way the Church is heading. When I was ordained in 1949, I very much wanted to celebrate my first Mass in the church of my local parish. It would have meant so much to me, for reasons which must be obvious. The request was turned down flat. There was no explanation, no discussion, no appeal. That's the way things were in those days – rampant, inflexible autocracy. And look at today's Church – in crisis.

The relics of the old ways are still to be seen. Go into any town or small village in Ireland and it's likely that the biggest building you will find there will be the Catholic church. Recently, I officiated at a funeral in Dublin. The church was colossal, of basilica proportions, reeking of ostentation. It was also empty. The tide has turned dramatically. The huge seminaries are echoing shells. Congregations have dropped away. I think the Church is beginning to lose its way, possibly because some clergy have started to ignore the calls on their compassion, and their duty to look after the flock is being pushed aside. It is beyond question that there have been many instances around the world of people ignoring the imperatives of natural justice. They have turned their backs on responsibility and have ended up materially advantaged. It has happened among the Catholic clergy no more, and certainly no less, than among any other social group. That is what occurs when social involvement is sacrificed on the altar of self-aggrandizement.

All of us in religion these days are more aware than ever that openness is essential. The shields of silence must be torn down in order to have a leaner, healthier, more honest and more humane Church. I truly believe that the Vatican museum should be sold; that any kind of set-up which allows Papal Nuncios to rule with such power should be abolished. When a hierarchical structure, with all its pomposity and formality, places more importance on rank, power and petty protocols than it does on people and their needs, people suffer and bureaucrats flourish. I know many religious people who have spent time overseas on missionary work, battling on their own initiative to get the job done – often in severe cases of poverty and isolation – who become disillusioned on their return home, because they are sucked into the voracious gullet of Church bureaucracy, with its many regulations and its resultant frustration. You learn to live with it, or else you leave.

I know exactly what it feels like. You find yourself trying to fit into 'the system' somehow, but 'the system' is uncomfortable with you, it wishes you were somewhere else. So you just learn to live with it, as I did many years ago. It never gets any easier. But I am a priest because a priest is what I wanted to be since I was a boy, and a priest is what I intend to remain until I die. A Connemara man once told me, 'They're not going to wrench the hand of Christ from me.' Nor from me either.

5

'THE PLAY'S THE THING...'

Apart from the practical problems on the island which needed to be solved, I began to be increasingly worried about the Mass itself. Although the few minutes at the end of Mass were successful in spurring the congregation on, many were still too silent during the actual service. They wouldn't open their mouths. They wouldn't say the responses aloud. Certainly, they stood up and knelt at the appropriate moments, but otherwise – nothing.

More than anything, I wanted the congregation to understand the beauty of the Mass; I wanted them to see that it was a celebration, a chance to offer God a gift – a gift that constituted our love, thanks and our prayers asking for forgiveness and help. The Mass is an opportunity for the congregation to make its presence felt; here on Tory, however, it wasn't much of a celebration. There wasn't even any singing, and I knew full well that they could sing. The island has a rich tradition of music and song, and I had heard them singing on other occasions. But in St Colmcille's there was an unnerving silence, not even a note or the slightest indication that they were a part of what was going on. How to start a blaze in their involvement? How to triumph over any encroaching sense of my own helplessness or incapacity to do it?

The solution actually emerged through the discovery of another problem. I found out that although there were island children who needed to be taught, and a school in which they should be taught, the teacher – Mary Colgan – had left, apparently after a dispute with my predecessor.

I was in *teach sagairt* one day at the end of September, when someone knocked on the door.

'*Tar isteach*,' I called out, 'come in.'

The door opened and a very shy-looking woman came into the room.

'I'm Mary Colgan,' she announced, 'the teacher.'

'I'm very glad to see you,' I said. 'Sit down, sit down, *suidh síos*.'

Mary poured out her story to me. She had come to the island from the Midlands about a couple of years prior to my arrival, and had fallen in love with it. She never intended to leave, but the bitterness of the row between herself and the former curate had been enough to force her to leave, giving no indication as to when – or indeed, whether – she would be back.

The pull of the island had been so strong, however, that she had come back to the county, taking lodgings in a house not far from Magheraroarty. It was there that she picked up the local gossip relating to Tory, and discovered that the former curate had been replaced by a Jesuit from Dublin, who claimed he'd just gone there to learn the language. So she stayed around for a couple of weeks, monitoring the talk, and eventually decided to come out and see for herself what was happening.

'What I heard about you didn't seem too bad,' she smiled, 'so here I am.'

I'd established from some of the islanders that Mary had a great voice and was a fine singer.

'I'm glad you came back, Mary,' I said, 'and I hope you'll stay, because we need you, the children need you.'

'We'll see how things go, Father. I'm not promising anything.'

I turned away from her for a moment, took a deep breath, turned back to her and said, 'You're the answer to my prayer. Mary, not only must you come back and take charge of the school again, I want you to take charge of the church choir.'

She was taken aback, and just looked at me without answering.

'And don't tell me there are no singers on the island, Mary,' I continued, 'because I know that there are.'

'There are indeed, Father,' she agreed, '*beautiful* singers.'

Within a few days, Mary Colgan went back to teaching again, took on the responsibility for the choir, and did wonderful work at both jobs. She was delighted to be back. The Mass that she taught the choir to sing was the loveliest that I've ever heard. Both children and adults were encouraged to join, and they sang *as Gaeilge* – in Irish. Occasionally Mary, or one of the members of the choir, would come to me and say deferentially: 'Father, there's a nice hymn we used to sing, and we were wondering if–'

Every time it happened I'd cut them short and say, 'Look, you don't have to come and ask me, you don't have to ask for permission – just sing whatever you want to sing.'

As a result, I never knew from one Sunday to the next what I was going to hear, but that only made it more exciting. I always loved what they sang. The people flowered. They were appreciated and reacted accordingly. Being appreciated seemed to be a new experience for them, and the music and song they introduced into the Mass were unlike anything I had heard before. The music always moved me deeply, even on those occasions when I didn't understand all the words. It was as if they were singing their lives, singing the island, making the rock come alive. Mary taught the choir to sing *a capella* (unaccompanied).

Occasionally, a remembered sorrow would be described by repeating the word *ochón*. This is a one-word lamentation, which
translates roughly as 'woe' or 'woe is me!'. It's a keening sound,
sometimes eerie in its effect, which is a natural bewailing expression or sound for people experiencing or identifying with things
that touch their emotions.

When, eventually, I succeeded in encouraging them to join in
the bidding prayers, I knew I had a notable success on my hands.
At first they were hesitant, unsure and shy; they mumbled a
phrase in a voice that could barely be heard. But as they drew
strength from one another and grew in confidence, they began to
speak up and let themselves be heard. The intentions they mentioned often focused on their needs, the needs of the community,
the dead, and the world's many problems. I remember one day
thinking that with this kind of strength behind them, they could
go through anything, and so could I. Their faith was as solid as
the rock on which they lived.

I consecrated Tory Island to the Sacred Heart during Holy
Hour, inspired by the life of St Margaret Mary Alacoque (1647–
1690), a French nun of the Visitation Order who told her Jesuit
spiritual director, Fr Claude La Colombière, about her visions of
Christ, and thus spread a public devotion to the Sacred Heart
which was to become part of every Jesuit's life from the seven-
teenth century to the present day. I followed this by instituting
First Friday devotions and the Holy Hour. (Making the 'First Fri-
days' is the voluntary devotional custom of receiving Holy Com-
munion in the first Friday of each month for nine consecutive
months. Historically, practitioners were expected to spend a 'holy
hour' in the presence of the Blessed Sacrament each Thursday,
and to celebrate annually the Feast of the Sacred Heart.)

Tory Island has a wealth of traditions handed down over the
centuries, and I was happy to see that they continued to be

performed. They embraced song and dance, and didn't attack, erode or impinge upon Christian belief in any way, so I was glad to see them being enjoyed. The islanders asked if they could incorporate their hymn-like songs into the Mass, and I was more than happy to let them. I saw it as a sort of liturgical development. Unfortunately, they were often seen as an easy target for cheap off-island remarks about superstition and paganism. 'A bunch of lazy, superstitious pagans is all they are,' was one description voiced to me by a diocesan priest. Many mainlanders on the Donegal coasts referred to them disparagingly as 'pagans'. Joe Murphy, writing in the *Irish Echo* in New York, said:

> One is told, don't go to Tory, the people are strange. They don't trust visitors. They're very superstitious. If a man was drowning, they wouldn't save him. They say the sea must claim its dead.

The islanders were well aware of this appalling slander on their character, and the derision with which some mainlanders treated them. But I supported them all the way. Like any other community, not everyone was equipped with first-class theological knowledge, but they knew the Ten Commandments, and the basic tenets of the Christian faith. Their belief in Christ and his Word was absolutely unshakeable.

I felt proud to be part of a community which, many centuries before, had been evangelized by the indefatigable Colmcille. On the island, he and his monks were able to devote themselves to a life of holy seclusion. Whilst I didn't feel I was secluded from the real world, on those long walks around the island, when I went to Colmcille's tower to pray, touching the stones for comfort and inspiration, I liked to think that he would have understood and empathized with our struggle.

Winter, with its short, melancholy days and bitter, harsh weather, had the island in its grip; my first Christmas on Tory was approaching fast. Nothing I had experienced before could have prepared me for a Tory winter. Every night the wind screamed and hammered at the windows; sometimes I even wondered whether the glass would be able to withstand the attack much longer! What complications and difficulties would it bring with it and leave behind, I wondered. I always sought refuge in the words of John, the apostle, whenever even the slightest trace of trepidation grew in me. 'There is no fear in love, but perfect love casts out fear' (1 John 4:18); 'If the Son therefore shall make you free, ye shall be free indeed' (John 8:36). How could I not be buoyed up with such tremendous thoughts to carry me?

I ordered a big Christmas tree on the mainland and made arrangements for it to be brought out to the island.

'Where are you going to have it set up, Father?' Jimmy Duggan asked me when he heard about it.

'Outdoors,' I said, 'where it'll be visible.'

'*Outdoors*?' asked Pádraig in disbelief. 'In this weather? It'll be blown to hell and back again.'

'Well, sure we'll try it anyway,' I shrugged.

What problems the ferrying of the tree caused the boatmen I was never told in any great detail, but it can't have been an easy trip. Sudden bursts of wind wrenching at the boat's unaccustomed additional bulk of trunk and branches must have been awkward for the helmsman. I found it better not to dwell on it; I just prayed for its safe delivery.

When the tree finally arrived, I got a few of the men to erect it outside *teach sagairt*, anchoring it in position with wire, rope and string. When they'd finished tying it down, Pádraig said, 'I *still* think it'll be blown to hell and back!'

But it wasn't, and it looked brave and fine, that Christmas tree of ours standing out in the elements on an island where no trees grew. When we strung it with coloured Christmas lights which danced in the wind, it radiated a happiness all of its own.

That first Christmas was magical. The singing at Midnight Mass was exquisite. The nostalgia induced by the thought of the dying year, as well as memories of Christmases past and friends, colleagues and family, was made more intense by the choir's voices blending in harmony.

'Oiche Ciúin,' they sang, 'Silent Night'. I was moved to tears, and silently offered my thanks to God.

'Help me to keep going,' I prayed. 'Don't let me get afraid. Don't let me get tired. Don't let the frailties take over. We're all in *your* hands, Lord, whatever is going to happen is going to happen. With your help we'll try to endure it.'

On Christmas Day I was treated to a delicious dinner, cooked for me by Mary McGinley, my housekeeper. A 17-year-old island girl, she was a smiling, good-natured human whirlwind who came in for a few hours every day. Whenever she was about the place, you couldn't feel down or depressed for long. With her marvellous laugh and her innate sense of mischief, allied to her inclination to play small practical jokes, she was, as they say in the country, a tonic.

I sat by myself in the little dining room and ate my dinner, alone with my thoughts about Christmas and all that it represented. When I had cleared away the dishes, I put on my heavy coat and went out to one of the neighbouring houses where I was made warmly welcome. I sat among them for hours, enjoying the *ceól agus craic agus rinnce*, their singing and stories and dancing. They had preserved and maintained in full vitality the Gaelic culture to which they and all the Irish are heirs. It was a fitting and beautiful end to my first Christmas on the island.

When I eventually left in the early hours of the morning, the wind had shifted and there were the signs of a storm blowing in from the ocean. I realized that the worst of the winter weather was still to come, and began to reflect upon what the islanders would have to look forward to in the coming months. An idea began to dawn on me which would help solve two problems at once.

The islanders, understandably when considering their despicable treatment, had become increasingly lacking in confidence when it came to dealing with the mainlanders. They knew what the island needed to make it viable for habitation, but they had lost the confidence to make themselves heard and be listened to. They knew, therefore, that the bureaucrats could afford to ignore them. It was essential, however, that they learn how to speak up for themselves. What better way than a drama group? This could be a challenging and entertaining way to pass the winter nights, as well as allowing them to develop their skills in public speaking. Just as Jesus made extensive use of parables, I thought that the islanders could write about *their* life experiences, feelings and opinions on matters important to them, and then gradually develop these into actual plays.

I knew very little about plays and nothing at all about playwriting. I had a vague knowledge of *Everyman*, that most famous of all the medieval morality plays, but the emphasis would be on 'vague' and not on 'knowledge'. I didn't even have the remotest notion of how one goes about setting up a drama group; I knew nothing about dialogue, characterization, plots, props, entrances, exits, scenes, acts, stage directions, make-up, lighting, costumes. But, as usual, I didn't worry about it, I simply took the most direct route.

'Jimmy,' I said one day to Jimmy Duggan, 'I had a dream last night.'

'Did you, Father?' he replied. 'And are you going to tell me what was in it?'

I hadn't had any dream at all, but I pressed on.

'Well, we wrote our own drama. Look, we've been waiting around long enough, and we can't seem to get any books in to get a drama going. Maybe it's providential; maybe God wants us to write our own?'

It was intended to be a question, to elicit a response from Jimmy. Silence.

'I wonder, could we have a go?' I pressed.

'Cripes, Father, I can barely write me name!' Jimmy laughed.

'Will you come around tonight, and get Gráinne to come, too? We'll have a chat about it then.'

So Jimmy rounded up a few others, as well as Gráinne (his wife), and that evening we sat in front of a good fire and I explained my 'dream' to them in more detail. Then I went around the group, handing each person a pencil and paper before returning to my own chair.

There was absolute silence in the room. The only sounds to be heard were when a sod of burned-out turf collapsed into the centre of the grate, sending a small shower of tiny sparks up the chimney. Otherwise, nothing. No one opened his or her mouth, and I didn't feel like being the one to start the ball rolling. It was up to them.

Still nobody spoke. They sat, pencils in hand, looking down at the blank sheets of paper. It was painful. Eventually I said, 'For goodness sake! What kind of a crowd are you at all? What are we doing? We're supposed to be writing a drama. *I* don't know anything about it, *you* don't, but we have to *try*. Anyway, it'll have to have a title, a name, won't it?'

I thought quickly.

'Jimmy,' I demanded, 'what are you?'

'A fisherman,' he replied.

'Right, put it down quick,' I said. '*An t'iascaire* – "The Fisherman" – that'll be the name of it.'

And that's how we started. There were many nights during the gestation period of the play when we worked to the background noise of screeching squalls and howling gales – Tory's usual winter weather. But we were on land and indoors, warm and secure from the tumultuous seas as we turned our efforts towards creating a play about our island.

It was amazing to watch the way the group set about the task. Sometimes they argued volubly. Sometimes they laughed in amusement or derision. Each put forward ideas, which were listened to, evaluated, praised or ridiculed, adopted or rejected. Little by little the play grew and developed. To me, it was almost a miracle – these islanders, so mute at Mass when I first arrived, were now loud, enthusiastic and totally released from all inhibitions! They called me the producer, but I'd never produced a play in my life! We named ourselves '*Cumann Drámaíocht Oileáin Tóraigh*' – the Tory Island Drama Group.

During one of our regular meetings to discuss the play, Jimmy Duggan came in and announced, 'I had a dream last night.'

'Did you, Jimmy?' I grinned, echoing what he had said to me previously. 'And are you going to tell us what was in it?'

'I had a dream,' he said, 'and there was a song in it from long ago. Will you all listen to it? It's called "*Seán Bán mo Grádh*" – "John, my fair-haired love". '

He began to sing it. Jimmy had a lovely singing voice, and he sang now with great feeling, everyone in the group listening with rapt attention. When he finished there was a round of applause which Jimmy acknowledged shyly. After a while he tentatively asked, 'Could we maybe use that in the drama?'

The song was about a Tory custom, that just before a wedding, the prospective bride and groom would attend a special party which was also attended by the older women of the island, all of these women being required to sing a song. One of the twists in

'*Seán Bán mo Grádh*' was that the lover of one of these women also happened to be the prospective bridegroom. Not only that, but the woman in question was pregnant. Depending on how well she sang the song – a lament – the prospective bridegroom might leave the prospective bride, and return instead to his (pregnant) first love.

Jimmy's suggestion started off another round of discussions and exchanges of suggestions and ideas. Notions which had been accepted were now either ditched or amended. In the end the consensus, largely influenced by Pádraig Mac Rúairí's powerful and eloquent persuasion, was that not only should the name of the play be altered to that of the song, but that certain elements contained in the song should be incorporated into the play itself.

I was secretly delighted that the drama they had chosen to act reflected island customs, beliefs and life. I really believed in the power of drama to get a message across and, in particular, the power of plays to show something of the true nature of those who write them, and to give a mirror image of the communities they are written about.

Before we could actually perform the play, though, we had to deal with another problem. Where would the audience sit? We had no chairs in the hall. A request to *Roinn na Gaeltachta* for £100 to buy the necessary chairs didn't materialize. So, the challenge was put to the islanders: to make the chairs themselves. First of all, we needed some money. For that, I turned to the Lions Club in Dublin. (Lions Clubs are part of one of the world's largest service club organizations; non-political, non-sectarian and dedicated to promoting civic improvements, education, health and international co-operation.) I was given the opportunity to talk at one of their meetings about the threat to Tory Island. As Des Nix, columnist for the *Sunday Press*, described it,

I 'walked into a Dublin hotel … tucked into a fine lunch, regaled [my] hosts with stories … and left with £350 and the goodwill of the donors.'

I was delighted with such a spontaneous, generous contribution. Interestingly, Des Nix actually described this gesture as a sort of 'offer of compensation for the years of official neglect which now threatens the whole future of the 200-strong community'. Whatever motive they had, I had no qualms about accepting any form of assistance which would better the lot of the islanders. With the £350, I bought a mobile welding machine and the necessary steel in Dublin and brought them back to Tory. Then, members of the Government self-help group FAS came to Tory to train six volunteers in making tubular, steel self-stacking chairs. They did it! With no distractions, they were focused on the job and a few hundred chairs were made. As to their quality, a major store in Sligo tested and examined them. Their verdict gave the thumbs up to the project saying the chairs were of better quality than their own, and just as cheap at only £10 each!

So we were all set to stage our production. When we finally put on 'Seán Bán mo Grádh' in the hall in January 1981, the audience loved it. As someone remarked to me: 'That rang bells all over the island, Father.'

I later found out that a Gaelic Drama Festival was to be staged at the *Amharclann Ghaoth Dobhair* (the Gaelic theatre) in Gweedore, Co. Donegal, at the end of March 1981. When I announced to the group that we would enter for it, there was some hesitation. Sensitive to the derision with which some mainland people treated them, they were a little unwilling to go. But when the time came for them to put on 'Seán Bán mo Grádh', they gave it everything, despite the hall being only half full.

When the performance finished, the adjudicator, Lorcan O' Riain from Belfast, came towards me. I must admit I was slightly worried myself – was he about to laugh us out of court and pour scorn on our efforts?

'Father,' he said, 'that was altogether astonishing. I've never seen anything like it. It broke every rule in the book, mind you, but it is so *real*. Gut community drama, that's what it is. For God's sake don't change it – develop it.'

Our home-made play won first prize in the festival, and O'Riain, in his closing speech, called it 'unique'. Afterwards, we received a request to put on a repeat performance at Gweedore. This time, playing to a full house, the reception the audience gave the Tory islanders was loud and long and enthusiastic. The transformation of the group was amazing, the delight at being applauded by the mainlanders clearly showing in their faces. The many winter nights spent working on the play in *teach sagairt* had been worth it. Other public performances followed, at Falcarragh and Magheraroarty. *Cumann Drámaíocht Oileáin Tóraigh* had arrived. It was written about and spoken about for weeks afterwards.

The achievements exceeded anything we had hoped for. On Tory, the drama group's mainland success was treated and greeted with pride. New hope began to flower. I got a great boost from the whole exercise because it provided evidence that it was genuinely possible to get the people off the ropes and out again into the centre of the ring, fighting.

6

TAKING ON THE BUREAUCRATS

Roinn na Gaelteachta, the government agency which dealt with all Irish-speaking communities, could often appear untouchable – especially since no public representative was speaking up for the island's small population. I felt that it was doing the bare minimum for Tory, that it didn't really care.

It was time to change that picture. I started to pester *Roinn na Gaelteachta* with letters and phone calls, because I wanted to make sure that they were fully aware of how the islanders really felt. It was essential, however, that the department officials heard the islanders' voices as well as mine, so I requested a meeting in Dublin at which a deputation from Tory, led by myself, would appear. My request was granted – reluctantly, I felt – and I was asked precisely how many would be in our party. I did a quick mental calculation and quoted a number, wondering why the question had been asked. At a meeting of the Co-op that evening I told them what I had arranged and said, 'We're going up to Dublin to meet those lads and tell them a thing or two.'

Having been lucky with the weather, we were able to get off the island on schedule to begin the long drive south-east to Dublin. Before going into the meeting, I gathered the islanders around me on the pavement. They were a bit uptight about what was bound to be somewhat of an ordeal, and I wanted to try to relax them.

'There's no need to be worrying about this,' I said. 'They're just people, and we're people, but don't let's mess up the opportunity. Now, at the beginning *I'll* say something, and whatever I say, for God's sake don't you say exactly the same! Say something else, *anything* else. You know what you feel – well, *express* it, whatever comes into your head. Talk. All right?'

There were nods all round.

'OK, come on, let's go in – and good luck.'

When we were shown into the meeting room, it was obvious straightaway from the arrangement of the chairs and tables that this was to be a formal affair. The department officials all sat together behind a table facing a group of chairs laid out for us, as if we were their audience, or – more accurately – as if we were in a courtroom. As we took our places, I thought: it's like going on trial – but for what? For speaking up? I counted the officials. They outnumbered our party by *one* – I now knew why I'd been asked how many were in our group. Their number had been chosen deliberately.

The *Rúnaí* (secretary) opened the meeting by saying, '*Dia dhuit, a Athair, agus na daoine anseo, fáilte rómhaimh*' – 'Hello, Father, and members of the delegation. Welcome. Well now–'

I lost no time at all in going into my introductory remarks. I was short and to the point. I was astonished, however, when one official immediately criticized the quality and paucity of my Irish, as if he were trying to discredit me in front of the islanders. I explained that the very reason I went to Tory in the first place was to learn Irish, but they wouldn't listen. The officials informed us that they *knew* what they were doing, that they had jobs to do and did them absolutely correctly; how dare *I*, who had only just come on the scene, criticize *them*.

The vituperation was like stinging acid. I glanced around at the islanders. Some of them were open-mouthed. One or two of them looked frightened. But what looked like anger could be seen mounting in the faces of the others.

Turning back to the officials, I quietly said, 'All right, don't listen to *me*. Listen to *them*. Yes, I've only been on Tory Island a short time, and I still don't know the whole story. But I know enough of it to justify our being here. Listen to *them* – they've lived their whole lives on the island.'

Jimmy Duggan stood up and began to speak in his beautiful, eloquent Irish. He had only just started, though, to put forward the islanders' case when one of the officials interrupted him, roaring, '*Ráiméis*! Rubbish!'

The look on Jimmy's face was one of shock and outrage, but the rude interruption only acted as a catalyst for the others. Suddenly Pádraig was on his feet, holding his hand up for silence.

'I'm Pádraig Mac Rúairí, from Tory Island,' he said in a loud, firm voice. 'They know me there as the *Dramadóir*, the dramatist. But I can tell you, this is no acting – this is for *real*.'

When he sat down, accusations and counter-accusations flew between the department officials and the islanders. Some of it was in Irish so swiftly spoken and shouted, and with such emotion, that I couldn't understand all the words. But there was no mistaking the intentions. It was as if the fury engendered by decades, maybe centuries, of being discriminated against, had at last risen to the surface.

When all of them had had their say and the meeting was over, I led them out of the room and out into the street. I was very proud of them, and I told them so. They had had a rough ride, but refused to be petrified. They'd given just as much as they got – maybe more. Their frustrations were out in the open now, no longer buried under layers of inhibition.

'Did we do all right, Father?' they asked.

'You were terrific,' I said.

Then they began to recall various bits of the exchanges, a couple of them actually hugging with unrestrained glee.

'Did you see the look on that man's face when Pádraig said that thing about it not being acting?'

'Oh God will you ever forget it? That was telling them!'

'And when you said…'

'And when you told them…'

The conversations about the meeting continued on our way back to Tory Island. One thing was certain: *Roinn na Gaelteachta* now knew for sure that the Tory Islanders weren't passive any more. They were no longer a pushover.

I now turned my attention to the media. Using the media was something that I knew would work. Indeed, in 1973, Fr Pedro Arrupe (former General of the Society of Jesus) advocated that Jesuits should learn how to use it; that the mass media should be part of the Jesuits' apostolate. If the Lord gives you the ammunition to get on with the job, I reasoned, you get on with it. If the ammunition isn't readily available, you manufacture it. Using the media was my manufactured ammunition. I decided to indulge in the ancient activity of pamphleteering; whatever that decision would bring down on my head, I reasoned, so be it.

I took heart in the story of Fr James J. O'Donnell, former Parish Priest of Tory. On 20 December 1882, he wrote a letter to the Editor of *The Universe* which described the '300 individuals in utter distress' living on Tory. He described how inaccessible the island was during the winter months; for example, he wrote that

'In November we were three consecutive weeks without communicating with the mainland. In that storm, I was obliged to beg this winter store of provisions from the lighthouse keepers, and give it to my poor people to keep them alive.' His views on the help the islanders were given by the local government were strangely familiar: 'Government has refused to do anything for them except to leave them to the death that threatens them, so that nothing now remains to them but to cry for aid to a charitable public.'

He wrote to various newspapers, describing the appalling situation on Tory – the lack of food, in particular:

> seaweed mixed with a little rye crushed between two rough stones was the only food on the island. With such diet for sick people, no wonder that death followed. Already three men have been laid to take their long sleep in the island cemetery, the victims of starvation.

However, O'Donnell was to find that some people's reaction was simply to feel that the situation had been grossly exaggerated – and I could empathize entirely with how he must have felt. When I began to write letters (and make phone calls, now of course!) to many different people, I received almost identical rebuffs and denials of reality. Fr O'Donnell was publicly rubbished in the newspapers, as I was to be. A pamphlet by Benjamin St John Baptist Joule (the owner of the island) even went so far as to accuse the islanders of cursing the lighthouse because it would diminish their spoils from wreckage! (At that time, there existed all around Britain a disreputable section of society, loosely known as 'wreckers', who lived off the spoils taken from ships wrecked on the coastline.) Fr O'Donnell was swift to defend his parishioners against any form of attack and the correspondence between himself and Mr Joule grew in ferocity.

It seemed that Fr O'Donnell and I had a great deal in common: we were prepared to stand up for what we believed in, whatever the cost. His newspaper campaign regarding the plight of the Tory islanders had been particularly effective, and I knew that mine had to be as well.

I didn't reckon on the force of the first newspaper headline, though: TORY ISLAND P.P. ACCUSES COUNCIL OF 'GENOCIDE'. It certainly grabbed the attention! The story carried by the *Derry People* and *Donegal News* was accurate enough (I was not, strictly speaking, a Parish Priest, but I wasn't complaining), but that word 'genocide' did it. In my pamphlets ('Tory's Horror' and 'The Scandal of Donegal County Council') I did accuse the County Council of 'carrying out a "genocide" policy against the islanders'. Not surprisingly, the Council did not want to comment on this.

From then on, press coverage of the situation on Tory increased quite dramatically. The *Donegal Democrat* columnist, Gerry Moriarty, wrote that 'where Donegal is the Cinderella county, Tory, isolated and neglected, is an abandoned child.' He actually contacted *Roinn na Gaeltachta* himself, and said:

If my own experience is indicative of how the Government feels about the crusading priest, he can justify his aggressiveness … When I spoke to an official, I found a reaction that was anything but accommodating: he wanted written questions submitted … I found this unusual as the queries were straightforward, and when I explained this and put the questions to him, he came back with an astonishing declaration: 'You are being used.' Certainly an over the top reaction for a civil servant. Father Ó Péicín came up against the same official wall many times.

John Healy of the *Irish Times* wrote that the litany of neglect was as old as it was familiar. Talking about the evacuation of islands such as Inishmurray, Achillbeg and the Blaskets he movingly wrote:

> ...*island people were able to cope with solitude. But when a strong neighbour, now feeble with the years, slipped into the tide, going to or coming from the mainland, the fear of an accidental death of a like kind was enough to encourage the last handful to leave the island forever.*

Regarding Tory, his view was that 'if the islanders feel sore that their voices do not always carry even as far as the mainland, let alone Dublin and to the seat of Government, then it is not the first community along the West coast, or off the coast for that matter, with that complaint.' Healy felt that no one would say outright that islands like Tory should be abandoned, 'no more than a politician will tell a village it has no future; you assure the people you'll do your best, but things can be difficult.' Identifying that Tory was in need of air as well as sea links, he said: 'The odds seem to be against them...'

Tim Jones of the London *Times* came across from England to do a feature article on the island. He quoted me as saying: 'Tory is a unique Gaelic community and, if it dies, a jewel of Irish culture will be gone.' One unexpected result of this particular article was a wonderful gift which was delivered courtesy of a Jesuit priest in Middlesex. A letter arrived one day from him, on behalf of his parish, which said that he had read the article in *The Times* about Tory, and that when he thought about the island's people arriving at St Colmcille's wet and cold, to be faced by even more coldness and dampness inside the unheated building, he wanted to do something to change things for the better.

He knew I was helpless in this matter. There was no heating system, nor was there any prospect of installing one. So he actually organized the purchase and shipping to Tory of a heavy duty industrial fan heater, a powerful and noisy piece of equipment which, if switched on half an hour before Mass, not only took the chill off the church's interior, but warmed it. It made St Colmcille's an infinitely more comfortable place for the congregation. Such a generous and kind action touched us very deeply. What he had done combined decency with sensitivity, and lifted all of us in our continuing fight.

It can be a surprising experience to come face to face with other people's perceptions of what you are and what you are like. I didn't realize that I would tend to be categorized by the press as being angry. But I had no quarrel with that – I was. But then I wanted Tory Island to live, not die. I'd go anywhere and do anything, speak to anyone if I thought it might ultimately benefit the island's people. I'd shake the begging bowl wherever and whenever I thought it was worth the effort. Even Ignatius of Loyola, the founder of the Jesuit Order, spent a year as a beggar at Manresa, from which stemmed his famous Spiritual Exercises. His constant injunction to 'find God in all things' was to help me enormously.

I expected that someone in clerical circles would pick up on the increasing coverage, but there was silence on that front. No official contact of any kind was made, not even an invitation for a brief comment. It was almost as if they wanted me to do nothing but say Mass, keep my head down and keep quiet, going along with whatever was decreed. I couldn't do that, though. I don't know whether some felt that whenever I publicly said something provocative, I was metaphorically lobbing a grenade in their direction. The way I saw it was that the actions I was taking were tantamount to shouting: 'The ship is going down! We're *here*, over here – will you do something, anything, *please*!' Silence. If someone lobbed a grenade in your direction, for example, would you stand still and wait for it to go off? Or would you run and hide? To me, it felt as if the clergy ran away and hid.

Because of the lack of public support from the Church for my work on Tory, I felt that I was slowly being ostracized and isolated from the fold. It was as if this blow-in Jesuit from Dublin were disrupting their cosy plans, with his principal aim of taking the word 'evacuation' out of Tory-related vocabulary. As Colman Mc-Carthy of the *Washington Post* wrote, 'Adversarial politics is new to the Catholic clergy of Ireland, where Church and State share the same pew.'

The increased publicity about Tory meant that we were visited far more often by various politicians, although actual results weren't always forthcoming. When politicans came across to visit the island, they travelled by helicopter – the only form of air-transport suitable for Tory. The islanders now were much more confident of talking openly to them, spelling out to them what the island's needs were, rather than holding back. It was such a shame that of those things promised to the inhabitants (particularly around election time) not many were fulfilled. The politicians' conspicuous lack of action on behalf of Tory underlined what I was convinced of – that it was a forgotten, ignored island when it came down to the matter of providing financial or other economic aid.

I hoped that external, independent voices which joined the debate could lend weight to our argument. Letters began to appear in our national newspapers, for example, that of Eamon Mac Murchú, from Co. Waterford. He wrote:

What a hullabaloo there would be if the Book of Kells were burned, or the Ardagh chalice were melted down. Yet these are only dead relics. Tory, with its language, is a living monument to the Ireland that we are all supposed to want. Are we now to allow the final nail to be driven into the coffin of a language that has been spoken in this country since before the birth of Christ, and which, until the middle of the last century, was the majority language? If Tory is allowed to die, let it be on the conscience of the powers that be. They will be execrated by history for it.

Notable amongst other voices was an English architect, Brian Anson, commissioned in 1981 by *Údarás na Gaelteachta* to prepare a social and environmental plan for the west Donegal area; whether this was as a result of my campaign, who knows? He publicly declared that his primary recommendation was to save Tory. He said:

Not only is there no need for Tóraigh *to be emptied of its community (and, once evacuated, it will never again be inhabited by an Irish speaking community) but, within the not-too-distant future, the Irish nation will profoundly regret its disregard for the social uniqueness of* Tóraigh.

He quoted Lewis Mumford, an American author on social problems: 'Western man not merely blighted every culture that he touched ... but he also robbed his descendants of countless gifts of art and craftsmanship, as well as knowledge passed on by word of mouth that disappeared with the dying language of dying peoples.' Anson's concluding words need no explanation:

*As an architect I'm expected to save Venice or some such 'major'
treasure. No, like Mumford, I believe that if Tóraigh dies I am
robbed, and my world is less. For Tóraigh, as its own traditional
song puts it, 'Níl se 'na lá; níl se 'n oiche' – 'It is not day, it is not
night, but it is the darkest hour'.*

7

PUTTING TORY ON THE MAP

Easter, the oldest and most important celebration of the Christian year, always makes finding God easy. Easter 1981 saw Tory Island blessed with sunshine that bathed everything in glorious, warming light. It's at times like these that you are tempted to wonder whether even Paradise could be more beautiful.

All the colours were enhanced – even the bogland looked breathtakingly attractive. The funny-looking puffins flew low over the sea, the black and white oyster catchers looked proud as well as dramatic, and the ruins of the ancient stone walls were warm to the touch instead of being cold and streaming with dampness. The whitewashed houses gleamed boldly, the brilliant red surrounds of the windows standing out prominently like welcoming signals, and the washing hung on lines stretched between spindly poles had the appearance of festive flags. For once, the sea looked neither alien nor threatening as it heaved gently in the sunlight.

At the Easter Vigil we blessed and lit the paschal candle, and members of the congregation held up lighted candles to proclaim that Christ is the light of the world. The two yellow beams from the island's lighthouse appearing in the sky that night seemed to me to be exceptionally bright.

And then on the Easter Monday we had one of those rare and wonderful happenings on Tory, the wedding of an island couple. The bride and groom, Bríd Rodgers and Michael Meenan, made a handsome, happy pair. Bríd was a bright, cheerful girl, and Michael (whose brother Anton is now one of Tory's most distinguished artists) was an energetic and affable young fisherman. Almost the entire population of the island turned out in the sunshine for the ceremony and the celebrations which followed. These, let it be said, went on for many hours and involved song and dance of a vitality and verve that the world at large would see for the first time many years later only in *Riverdance*, the spectacular stage show. The Rodgers–Meenan wedding really was something to savour – and it still is.

Time doesn't stand still, though, and with Easter and the wedding celebrations behind us, the pace of developments on Tory quickened. Praying for ideas, and picking them up from wherever and from whomsoever I could, I had set in train plans for some major undertakings: namely, organizing what I called a 'Tory Week' in Dublin, arranging what I would christen a '*Seachtain Mhór*', a week-long island festival on Tory itself and taking part in the *Oireachtas* Festival in Dublin.

Robin Fox, after describing what it is like on Tory when the seas are really high – the whole island drenched with salt spray, the piers awash, the houses threatened – described the island as being 'a monument ... to man's astonishing endurance'. Well, it was endurance, and – latterly – at a price, the price often being depression. The islanders knew that many mainlanders would tend to take them at their own (the islanders') evaluation of themselves, and had therefore begun to have the courage of their convictions in fighting for what they believed in. But I still wanted to organize events that would fire the imagination, and capture the essence of Tory and its people. The three cultural events would be a wonderful way to display that island spirit.

I proposed that the central element of the 'Tory Week' in Dublin (to be held May 1981) should be an art exhibition – island art. There is a strong tradition of art on Tory. The original island artists were the brothers James (Jimmy) and John Dixon, and James Rodgers. In time, others followed them, including Michael Finbarr Mac Rúairí, Seán Rodgers, Rúairí Rodgers, Anton Meenan and Patsy Dan Mac Rúairí. Derek Hill, a famous British painter, was a frequent visitor to the island and encouraged their work. The style of Tory Island art is commonly classified as 'primitive' or 'naive'. The paintings show aspects of the daily facts of life on the island – the ever-present sea, the storms, the boats, the houses, the landscape. They have the freshness and impact of work done by people who, in the early days, had no television to influence them and no pictures to copy from. I hadn't been in Tory long when I discovered the work of Jimmy Dixon. Jimmy had died about a quarter of a century before I arrived. Grace, his sister, was the only surviving member of the family. I don't pretend to know much about art, but when I first came across one of Jimmy's pictures, I knew I was looking at something quite extraordinary. Grace told me that Jimmy was forever saying that he just painted Tory as he saw it. But if that was true, then Jimmy was seeing things in a way no one else saw them. He had visions of the future as well as images of the present. There was something prophetic about some of the pictures he painted.

Grace was in the twilight of her life when I met her. I used to call round in the evenings, and together we'd walk through her beautiful garden, a riot of colour from which most of the flowers were taken for the altar at St Colmcille's. We'd sit for hours talking about the old days when Jimmy and his brother John used to row to and from the mainland in their currach with the mail. It was enough of an ordeal in an engined half-decker. What must it have been like in their light, frail craft?

Talking to Grace about Jimmy and his work planted the seeds of the art exhibition idea in my head. It was a crazy idea at the time, when you bear in mind that I hadn't got the slightest inkling about art exhibitions and all the work they entail, especially when we had such a distinct lack of funds! All I knew was that a week-long exhibition in the capital would be a great awareness raiser, and something for the islanders to look forward to and prepare for.

I went about my preparations in my normal fashion – going straight to the top. I managed to arrange an interview with a Mr Finlay, the Chairman of the Bank of Ireland, at their headquarters in Dublin. He sat and listened patiently as I described my plan – hardly a model of conciseness or clarity – which was that I hoped to put on public display in Dublin a collection of paintings depicting life on Tory and other offshore islands, and to have some islanders – even some of the painters themselves – in attendance, so that they could answer any queries about Tory that might arise. Was there any chance, I wondered, that the Bank's beautiful, new exhibition area on the ground floor of their headquarters could be made available to us?

He asked me just a few questions and quickly made his mind up. 'Father,' he said, 'it's all yours.'

I couldn't thank the Chairman enough for his understanding and willingness to help – it really was tremendous. The first, perhaps the major, hurdle had been cleared. The second was obtaining professional artistic help to ensure that the exhibition itself was properly organized. For this, I turned to Carl Otto Schander. Schander was a Swedish artist who passionately loved Tory Island

– even acquiring a house there! – who I'd met earlier in the year. He didn't let me down. He gave selflessly of his time, and his invaluable advice ensured the exhibition was beautifully arranged.

Publicity, I knew, was a must, a sheer necessity. Ostrich-like 'head in the sand' behaviour would get us nowhere and, in the broader context, could well encourage more official neglect; that, in turn, would accelerate the erosion of the islanders' new-found confidence, as well as further erode their precious assets of pride and strength.

Where once I would have hesitated to contact reporters for fear of being accused of being a self-publicist, now I immediately started to ring newspaper journalists and radio and television stations. To anyone who would listen I poured out everything I knew about Tory Island and the forthcoming exhibition at the Bank of Ireland's headquarters. I was lucky that there were many receptive ears among the journalistic fraternity; columnists and reporters covered the story carefully and sympathetically. 'IS-LANDERS INVASION!' was one of the leading headlines; the story told of 'beleaguered people from our most remote inhabited island' and their 'indefatigable' priest – if only they knew! What pleased me most was that as well as giving much-needed publicity to the exhibition, the article pinpointed the vital fact that the aim of the 'Tory Week' was to draw attention to the positive side of Tory life, and thus help the Tory folk be proud once more of their ancient traditions. And, of course, it would underline the fact that the islanders were under pressure to leave this beautiful place.

The Dublin 'Tory Week' exceeded all expectations. Charles Haughey, the then *Taoiseach* (Prime Minister) and well known as a patron of the arts, had accepted my invitation to perform the official opening of the exhibition, but at the last minute had to withdraw because of political business. He therefore nominated Jim Tunney, a senior politician in the *Fianna Fáil* party, to take his place. We were pleased to have Jim with us, and his speech was, as usual, elegant and scholarly. The assembled crowd, which included the poet Seamus Heaney, warmly applauded him. A group of islanders was present, answering with dignity many questions about Tory and the effects that leaving the island would have on their lives. We received excellent media coverage; from that came the satisfaction of knowing that Tory was being noticed, talked about, spoken of, reported on. It all increased the community's chances of survival. We were far from being in an ideal situation, but we were making headway. From my own life experiences, I realized that in an emergency, if you wait around expecting ideal co-operation, ideal helpers and ideal responses to come forward, you'll be wasting your time. You have to get on and use whatever's at your disposal. We made that exhibition happen, and it helped our cause enormously.

I gradually learnt that sometimes it was necessary to 'cut the coat according to the cloth', and the music festival we organized for Tory is a good example of this. My proposed week-long celebration actually turned out to be a weekend festival which took place at the end of August 1981 – but what a weekend! Rough seas in the days preceding the *Seachtain Mhór* meant that the festivities were in danger of cancellation or, at the very least, being postponed. Nevertheless, the preparations went ahead. Our excitement and sense of anticipation grew, and volumes of prayers ascended heavenwards, heavily laced with entreaties to let the weather improve. And it did; instead of the sun darkening and the earth trembling, nature was at its most benign.

We had let it be known that Tory Island would welcome as many visitors as cared to come; little did we know from how far afield they would come – from all over Europe, 4000–5000 people arrived by the boatload, most of them for the first time. There was plenty for them to be entertained by and participate in. The big attraction of the weekend was the performance of Clannad, the folk group based in Gweedore, who were already major figures in the music world. Their performance on the Saturday night saw the huge crowd applaud with shouts of acclaim and handclaps that left fingers and palms stinging and sore. There was also a sports programme, a fireworks display, the Festival Mass, a tug o' war, a half-decker race from *Tor Mór* (the gigantic rocky outcrop on the eastern end of Tory) to the quay, *céilís* (dances) and *seisiúns* (musical get-togethers, where people dance, sing and have instrumental sessions). Over a thousand meals were prepared and served by the Women's Committee set up specifically for the festival.

Tory Island's first festival was a roaring success. News of our fight to save the community spread even further afield, as the islanders spoke to the visitors about their life, their fears for the future and their desire to stay. It was a marvellous opportunity to give the lie to those stories circulated about Tory by some mainlanders. Perhaps a truer picture of the Tory I knew can be seen in the words of Joe Murphy, the American journalist, which aptly sum up the kind of welcome that met the visitors that weekend:

It's only four o'clock, but the shop is soon full as the accordion's tones tell of the seisiún *in progress. Babies asleep upstairs cry, but are soon downstairs bouncing on their young mothers' knees in time to the music. Do we care? Do we prefer to romanticize things past, rather than love things present? Are we to leave this battle to a small band of kinsfolk who live their lives out on the stormy hard shoulder of Ireland. These proud people need help.*

Well, with articles like that, we did get help. In October, we were to highlight our cause even further with our participation in the *Oireachtas* Festival in Dublin.

The *Oireachtas*, promoted by *Conradh na Gaeilge* (the Gaelic League), is the major annual Irish cultural festival. It was founded towards the end of the nineteenth century by, among others, Dr Douglas Hyde (President of Ireland 1938–1945). Throughout his life, Hyde was prominent among those trying to preserve the Irish language; he was a prime mover in urging the Irish people to assert their separate cultural identity. The *Oireachtas* was dedicated to the de-Anglicization of Ireland through the revival and preservation of Irish as a spoken language.

I suggested that we enter a group, and particularly wanted Jimmy Duggan to sing the marvellous piece, '*Maidrín a rúa*' ('Little Red Fox'). This was an intricate, astonishing performance. Jimmy would first sing, unaccompanied, a song about a fox; then, to helter-skelter button accordion accompaniment, he would dance at furious speed, acting out the heart-thumping, ground-pounding fox chase. To watch it was to experience it, and to experience it was to be left breathless and exhausted, filled with wonder at his natural talent.

When I first spoke about the idea to Jimmy, his reaction was one of extreme caution. There was a shyness in him that I had to overcome. As I carried on talking to him as persuasively as I knew how, all the time appealing to his island pride, all the time scanning the rugged landscape of his face, I saw the initial hesitation beginning to melt.

'The islanders mustn't continue to be discouraged. You can't *not* go to Dublin, Jimmy,' I said. 'The *Oireachtas* is a platform. Climb up on it! Then maybe a whole group of us can go. We can enter some competitions against the other *Gaeltacht* competitors.'

'I'll go, so,' Jimmy said at last, 'and I'll have a word with a few of the others.'

I also knew of a television programme that was being transmitted live, on which we'd be guests, perhaps being able to display our talents. It was a studio-based bilingual programme which focused attention on customs, culture, people and all things Irish. But Jimmy, with surprising firmness, had other ideas.

'I'm not taking part in that,' he said. 'No television. The others can do what they want, but I'm not having any part of that. If I'm going to Dublin, I'm concentrating on the *Oireachtas*. You've convinced me we should be represented there, and I'll give it my very best. But what I want is a better deal for Tory, and that's more likely to be got by doing something worthwhile like taking part in the *Oireachtas*, rather than by sitting in any old television studio and being clapped by an audience at an old entertainment show. I'm having no part of that!'

The force and dignity of his speech won me over.

About a dozen islanders travelled to Dublin in the week of the *Oireachtas*. I'll always remember the moment in Newman House on St Stephen's Green when Jimmy Duggan's name was announced as the winner of the *sean nós* (traditional singing and dancing) competition. He had beaten competitors from Kerry, Connemara, Cork, Meath and Donegal, the first time ever that the big prize for the most famous and most traditional of all the competitions had been won by a Tory islander.

He had spent himself emotionally. His life had known hardship, hope and purpose. And now to those qualities could be added that of grace.

'Jimmy,' I said, holding his hand, 'you did your bit for Tory. I can't thank you enough.'

'I did my best, Father,' was all he said.

The three big events which we'd completed had all furthered our cause considerably. In fact, the subject of Tory Island had begun to arise repeatedly at County Council meetings. At one such meeting in October 1981, the Council's Chairman, Deputy

Clement Coughlan, actually stated that the Tory islanders felt the County Council was putting them under pressure to move to the mainland. He tabled a motion on the needs and priorities of the islanders which referred in particular to such matters as the litter problem on the island, refuse collection and the contribution of the Council to roadworks.

Coughlan said that the islanders 'had the notion' that they had been neglected by the County Council. He said the Tory Island people felt that by virtue of their isolation, the Council had a policy of trying to move everybody from Tory. He also stated: 'It would be no great achievement for the Council to provide a refuse collection for the island, and to make a decent contribution towards the roads.' The people of Tory 'were not being given the assistance they should get from the Council' and the Council must 'face up to the fact that Tory had got little money from the Council and they should try and do a lot more for them in the coming years…'

Thank God, I thought, the message is getting home. Though I disliked the inference of the word 'notion', Deputy Coughlan's words did prove that the constant efforts to attract official attention to the island's needs and the islanders' rights were paying some form of dividend, even if only in the form of being publicised.

But, as always, we had to look to new ideas to help us in our fight. I began to wonder why, given the current situation with Tory, there never seemed to be any similar talk of evacuating the Aran Islands. I finally decided it had a great deal to do with a film made in 1934, a stirring documentary called *Man of Aran*. It was made by Robert Flaherty, an extremely well-respected documentary maker, particularly amongst his peers. He was already internationally famous for *Nanook of the North* (1922), which was about an Eskimo family, and *Moana* (1926).

I must admit I'd never heard of Flaherty or his films until I went to Inishmore to brush up on my meagre Irish. It was in the little hall which served as a cinema that I first saw *Man of Aran*, not long after I had arrived. I was told by many people that it was a mighty film, and I wasn't disappointed. Despite the small screen, scratchy old 16mm print and a distorting soundtrack, the effect was powerful. It showed starkly and dramatically what the life of the islanders was like, their eternal battles with sea and wind, their unending struggle merely to exist. It showed the dangers and nobility of that struggle. The film increased awareness of the Aran Islands all over the world, established them as primary tourist sites, and helped to ensure their safety from the evacuation process. As Flaherty put it, an Aran islander's independence was 'the most precious privilege he can win from life. [He] fights for his existence, bare though it may be.'

Tory Island, I reckoned, needed its own *Man of Aran*-type film. I hoped that the BBC, or some burgeoning young director in the Flaherty mould, would come to our island and do for us what *Man of Aran* had done for the Aran Islands. We were lucky. In 1981, an RTE television crew came to make an Irish language programme about the island. Their attention had been drawn to Tory by the mounting press coverage, and the programme would eventually be transmitted in the *Féach* ('Look') series in April 1982. Its title: *Tóraigh – an toileán dearmadta*; *Tory – the forgotten island*.

The dramatic opening shots showed the barrenness, the deeply indented fissured coastline, the ocean-battered cliffs and the spiky rock formations which give the place its alien-looking landscape. Part of an interview I had done was used as the voice-over at the start: '*Bhí me ag obair san Aifric…*'; 'I had been working in Africa…' The film graphically depicted scenes of island life: the ugly, rusting wreckage of a long-abandoned Mini Minor; the open drains; the scraped earth; the treeless landscape; the dilapidated, tufted, weather-scarred burial ground; a woman carrying a blue plastic bucket of water from a well to her home; the picking, pecking, searching hens; the dogs and old lobster pots and daubed walls; the upturned boats hauled ashore out of the tide; the blue-hulled 'Floredge' seen coming in alongside the quay with its small cargo of bread, drink, and yellow gas cylinders, then leaving again later with the empties; two men dragging their black currach, which they launched bow-first and rowed out to sea; even a snippet of our successful drama production.

The interviewer asked if I was *sásta*, satisfied, with the state of the island. I spoke the truth. I had no qualms about doing this, I knew it would again put the spotlight on people that maybe didn't want to be singled out, but it was all part of the fight for the community. I described the island, its heritage, its culture and its needs; I passionately defended the island against the threat of evacuation. There were beautiful shots of Pádraig Mac Rúairí, standing outside a lace-curtained window, flat-capped and anoraked against the biting wind, speaking of the island's association with Colmcille. Jimmy Duggan, his high-cheekboned face furrowed with seriousness, was interviewed, as well as Mary Colgan, the teacher, and several of the island's painters.

The film was well received and spread awareness of our situation even further. There were some in the Church and political circles, however, who saw it and were not pleased. Ausonius was right with his observation *veritas odium parit* – truth produces hatred. Storms of ill-feeling were gathering; what with those and the storms which the elements threw in our direction on Tory, life was more and more resembling an endurance test.

8

GETTING THE WATER
AND LOSING THE PEOPLE

When you first go into a shanty town, or a bush village, in Africa, for the most part you know the poverty you will encounter. You know that there will be no piped water, for example, and that the inhabitants will therefore have to collect their domestic water in buckets, old plastic jerrycans or whatever comes to hand, and carry it to their dwelling places. You don't expect to find that type of deprivation in Ireland in the last quarter of the twentieth century. But I did.

The well at West Town was about 300 yards from my house, along towards Colmcille's tower. Every morning, be it in hail, rain, wind, storm or sunshine, I would see the women and children making their way to the well carrying plastic buckets, and then going homewards with the brimming receptacles. I kept on making approaches to Donegal County Council to do something about it: I wrote, telephoned, cajoled, begged and pestered them. Most of my enquiries were answered by some version of 'Look, Father, we can't move, we can't do anything until the engineer examines the situation.'

It took months to get the engineer to come to the island. When he did eventually arrive, I found out that he was looking for a high location at which a reservoir could be constructed, so that the water supply could work on a gravity feed.

Actually getting further information out of the engineer proved more difficult; it was almost as if he resented being asked questions by me.

'How long will it be before the water scheme for the island will be completed?' I asked.

'It depends on when it's started,' he answered.

'Well, when do *you* think it'll be started?'

'It all depends.'

'On what?'

'All sorts of things.'

'Such as?'

'Well, cost for a start – look, Father, I'm very busy.'

'I know you're busy – but as far as this island is concerned, it's about time.'

He started to walk away, saying something about not having to listen.

'Excuse me,' I said, walking after him. 'I *want* you to listen. Now, you mentioned cost. How *much* will it cost?'

'About three times as much as it'd cost on the mainland.'

'And how much would it cost on the mainland?'

'About £40,000.'

'And you're telling me it'll cost three times that here? £120,000 – is that what you're telling me?'

'That's what I'm telling you. Well, maybe not £120,000 but well over a £100,000 anyway.'

'Hasn't the Department approved the installation of a water scheme for the island?' I pressed.

But I didn't get a reply to that question. The engineer walked away purposefully, muttering to himself about the sheer expense of transporting equipment, machinery and workers to and from the island. I had hoped that construction would begin when the engineer had been to see the situation, but I was wrong. I rang the Council again.

'The costs of this thing are going through the roof, Father,' I was told by one official when I started pressuring them.

In an instant I was furious. 'This has got to stop, *now*,' I said.

'What do you mean? Are you suggesting we abandon the water scheme?'

'No, I'm *not*, and you know it,' I shouted. 'This carry-on by *you* people has to stop. What are the costs running at now?'

There was the sound of papers being shuffled. '£110,000,' he said at last, 'and it looks as if that could well climb to around £120,000. But £110,000 is as far as we can fund it.'

'So there's a gap?' I said.

'There is.'

I took a deep breath and said, 'All right. I'll be back tomorrow. You say you want to close that gap, and once you close it you'll begin work, right? I'll be back tomorrow, and that gap will be closed.'

'I don't understand,' he said.

'I'll get the additional money somewhere, somehow. I'll get the £10,000 or so that's needed, and then will you, for the love of God, get this thing started and no more foosthering around?'

At that moment I hadn't much of an idea where I'd lay hands on the money. 'The Lord will provide' was a quotation I'd heard and used a thousand times. Well, I was going to put it to the test one more time. After some deliberation, I rang Directory Enquiries and asked for the number of VSI (Voluntary Service International) in Dublin. It was just a shot in the dark, but worth a try.

When I told the telephonist at VSI the purpose of my call, she put me through to a man who asked me if he could help me.

I said: 'I hope you can – I'm looking for a work camp, or a work force, or whatever the appropriate term is.'

'Well, that's what we're here for,' he said. 'VSI organizes that sort of thing all over the world.'

'Did you ever hear of Tory Island?' I asked him.

'Of course I have – how many people are you looking for, and for how long?'

This was great – thanks, Lord.

I ended up by getting two work parties of 15 people (men and women, from nine countries), each for a period of two weeks. From the army in Letterkenny I got a loan of bunk beds. Ranks, the flour-milling firm, gave me bags of flour. The local supermarkets on the mainland rallied around with food. We turned a decrepit old shed called *Teach Dearg*, the red house, into a reasonable hostel for the women, and a house at East Town into a men's hostel. One of the volunteers, a young Dutchman, took care of the wiring.

We fed and clothed the work parties, put on a *céilídhe* for them every night; and by day they worked like the proverbial Trojans, connecting up the dwelling houses to the water main which the contractors had laid with the help of the JCB. In the space of four weeks, the VSI parties did £12,000 worth of work. They were heroic.

All in all, it took about two and a half months for the whole project to be completed, involving the construction of a reservoir, the laying of pipes, the connecting up of the houses and the building of a pumphouse. When the houses had a piped water supply for the very first time, the joy of the women in particular was wondrous. No longer would they have to fetch and carry water from the well! No longer would they have to struggle with heavy containers and aching backs. A basic human need, to have fresh, running water – a facility enjoyed and taken for granted by the mainlanders – was now part of their lives. A new pride in the appearance of the island's houses emerged. Paint was bought for the doors and windows, and whitewash and bluewash for the outsides of the houses. From dark and dusty corners brushes were recovered, and old buckets and tins were dug out for painting duty once more.

Windows and doors were scraped, and undercoat applied, and other surfaces washed down ready to be painted. And when the painting was completed, many of the islanders turned their attention to the little patches of garden close to their houses. The earth was weeded and turned over, and new seedlings and bulbs put into the soil. All over the island you got this feeling of a place and a people experiencing new hope and new pride.

It spurred us on to think about and to try to solve another problem that urgently needed to be tackled: that of transporting the children to school and back (especially during the worst of the winter weather) and of providing transport for the elderly and infirm. Naturally, no solution was provided by those who decided what Tory would or wouldn't get in the way of facilities. On Tory, the only mechanical vehicles that moved were the few noisy, fume-spewing tractors, and anyone of a certain age who has hitched a ride on one of these, or bounced on the hard, unyielding floor of a trailer, knows a thing or two about discomfort!

I got a crazy idea. For years I'd been fascinated by the fleet of battery-driven, silent milk floats that ghosted through the streets of Dublin early in the mornings on their delivery runs. Why not, I thought, use the chassis, motor and batteries of a milk float, and somehow convert it all into a kind of bus? In that way we could similarly operate a low-cost scheme (particularly since the batteries could be charged overnight) and a reasonably speedy service. There was no harm in giving it a try, I reasoned.

I approached a Dublin-based dairy firm, Hughes Brothers, who agreed to provide a chassis. Then, I contacted an ANCO official (the government training and employment authority) in Bunbeg, Co. Donegal, and put my idea to him. He reacted with encouraging enthusiasm and in no time at all came up with sketches, and then detailed design drawings, right down to the cushioned seats. The milk float chassis was delivered to the ANCO workshop in Bunbeg, and work started in no time at all. The name of Ireland's national transport organization is CIE (*Corus Iompar Eireann*), so we decided – with a certain amount of tongue in cheek – to call our project CIT, or *Corus Iompar Toraigh*.

One day, on a visit to the mainland, I decided to drop in at the workshop to see how work was progressing. Inside, to my astonishment, I was introduced to a lady who was showing keen interest in CIT's first acquisition – she turned out to be the Chinese ambassador. She asked all sorts of questions about the milk float/bus, as well as about Tory Island and its people. Before she left, she said she would like to visit the island some day to see the place for herself, and to see the bus working. She was to prove as good as her word. Some months later, she made a private visit to the island; sadly, I was on the mainland at the time and so didn't meet her there.

In due course, the CIT bus was completed, loaded up on a trawler and taken out to Tory where it was received with delight and immediately pressed into service. We appointed Paddy Boyle as its first driver. For young and old, for as long as it lasted (for the best part of two years) it was a godsend.

The knitting factory was yet another example of the islanders looking to help themselves by beginning new projects. Early in 1981, John Molloy, a gifted weaver in Donegal, had written to me, sending his warm wishes and congratulations on our work, and pledging his support if he could help in any way. John had set up his own business, which had blossomed over time, eventually branching out from tweeds to handknitted sweaters. We became firm friends and exchanged ideas on many topics, including the possibility of starting up a knitwear factory. John, as ever, gave the most valuable help, always in a totally unstinting, encouraging way. By entering a local competition organized by *Údarás na Gaeltachta* (a section of *Roinn na Gaeltachta* which deals specifically with the promotion of industry in Irish-speaking areas), we won the second prize of £2,000, which we used to become a part of Corra Fashions, an enterprise the department had helped to set up in Carrick, North Donegal. Our thriving little knitting factory gave sorely-needed employment to a group of island teenagers and one adult, Gráinne McClafferty. They produced some lovely products – sweaters, cardigans, scarves, wool hats – in attractive designs, and of a quality which led to their export to many countries around the world.

When the factory eventually folded after a couple of years, due to bad financial advice, we were all heartbroken: it had been, in its own way, another little beacon of hope, another reason for justifiable pride.

But perhaps the most important area that needed to be looked at was communications. An improvement in transportation links between Tory and the mainland was fundamental to the regeneration of the island. In 1970, the Aran Islands had managed to acquire a much-needed airstrip, based on Inishmore. I knew that Tory also needed this facility desperately. The first action to be taken was to obtain the right piece of land. To do this I needed to persuade the eight legal landholders to agree to set aside the necessary area. (Fox describes the situation regarding land ownership particularly well: 'I have spoken continuously of someone "holding" a piece of land, because this seems to me a better way of describing it than speaking of ownership ... each claimant being a descendant of the original ancestor who held the land and who is recognized as the focal point of the descent-claim system.')

I eventually managed to persuade each of them to sign a document which would transfer unreservedly all their rights and titles to the proposed site for the airstrip to the Co-op. The site we were proposing to use was between West Town and the lighthouse.

An inspector from the Department of Transport visited the site, checked it, and approved in principle that Tory should have an airstrip. The only problem that we then faced was the lack of any connecting air-link on the mainland. I therefore started negotiations with Malinair Limited, a Scottish airline based in Glasgow, which had begun to operate a service out of Carrickfinn airstrip, linking Donegal and Glasgow.

Their Operations Adviser, Captain K. E. Foster, had been the Operations Director of Loganair for over 20 years, during which time he was responsible for the design and construction of many such airstrips on similar small islands throughout Scotland. He expressed an interest in the proposed Tory Island project and was willing to advise on the feasibility and cost of completing the airstrip so that we could approach *Údarás na Gaelteachta* with a positive scheme for connecting the island with Carrickfinn. Malinair were, in turn, interested in looking at the viability of providing services between Carrickfinn and Tory Island during the stop overs on the Glasgow-Carrickfinn scheduled service.

I even collected over 16,000 signatures from people all over Europe in the campaign for work on the airstrip to be started. But it was all in vain. Like so much else relating to Tory, this potentially vital plan was ignored and the airstrip was never built. Tory is still without an airstrip and air service between it and the mainland.

Island access was also seriously hampered by the lack of a proper harbour. The old rudimentary pier at Camusmore Bay was all but useless when the weather turned dirty, which was often. Jutting straight out into the sea, it provided no shelter when the wind was off the sea. That was why the island's boats had to be hauled in so frequently, and why they spent so many unproductive months each year high, if not dry, far above the tide line. No wonder the island was, at times, cut off for weeks during the violent winter storms.

What was desperately needed was a safe, sheltered place to moor the boats. But all our requests and petitions, all our pleading and arguing were in vain; the authorities told us it was too expensive and therefore not feasible. They wouldn't even build us a breakwater.

The infuriating thing was that a harbour could have been built relatively inexpensively. I had got to know about the 'Rock Box Principle' – a technique which entailed selecting an area on the coastline where the rock profile drives deeply to below low water. (There are many such places on Tory.) A large hole would be carved and blasted out of the coastline, so forming what the engineers term a 'rock box'. The front of it would be left in to keep the sea out. The harbour thus formed would provide maximum shelter.

It had been done elsewhere with conspicuous success, notably on the Hebridean island of Grimsay. For the system to have been utilized for Tory's needs, it would have required a willingness and a modicum of imagination among the bureaucrats who made decisions affecting the island. In this, as in so much else, they were found wanting.

I knew we still had a fight on our hands, that we had a long way to go, but at that stage I'd not really considered the possibility that any of the islanders would have to leave.

It came as a total shock, therefore, that day in November 1981 when I noticed some of the villagers walking round the island and looking broodingly at things that normally they would have walked past. I immediately sensed that something was wrong. People were looking at things and places most familiar to them, almost as if they were trying to imprint details of shape and colour on their minds. It can't have been long after that the phone rang: 'The first ten families are going next week,' I was told by Deputy Clement Coughlan. I was devastated. I'd been racing against time, and I'd lost.

The details hit home like a series of hammer blows: in all, 52 people would be leaving Tory, a quarter of its population; more houses would have planks and bits of board nailed across their doors and windows. The departure of 16 children meant that the school roll numbers would be halved; the choir would be hit; the little group of altar servers would diminish; the island would be emptier. It felt as if we, the remaining islanders, were on a boat that was holed and sinking, and yet unable to plug the hole.

The morning of their departure was desperate. Leaving the place you have always called home is a trauma that no one who hasn't experienced it can understand. A great, deep sadness hung over everyone. Many tears were shed.

The men and women, boys and girls, who were leaving tried to give the impression that they felt it was all for the best. But you had only to look at their faces and body language, to know that they were leaving their hearts on the island. As the half-deckers moved away from the slip and set off across Tory Sound, it felt as if part of our very being was torn away.

I looked at Jimmy Duggan, loyal, spirited, talented Jimmy, and at Pádraig Mac Rúairí, who had turned out to be such an inspiring and fine-minded friend, and saw the sadness in their faces.

'Well, Father?' Pádraig said.

For a moment I didn't know what to say. I looked after the half-deckers, already a long way in the distance. Then I turned to the two men whose anxious eyes were searching my face.

'Are we going to let this floor us, or get us down?' I asked quietly. 'No, we are *not*! Things might *look* impossible just now, but we're not going to capitulate. Are you with me?'

'By God, we are, Father,' Pádraig resolutely said.

'You can count on us,' added Jimmy, and I went into the church by myself, and prayed.

9

MAKING AN APPEAL
AND GETTING NOWHERE

I could have left Tory any time I wished. There was no contractual obligation to stay. I could have opted for a very nice, comfortable life just *talking* about injustice, the poor, the state of the Catholic Church and so on. I knew it would have suited a lot of people, clerical and lay, if I'd decided to pack up and get off the island. But where would that have left me in relation to the Jesuit's mission for the poor? I held Pedro Arrupe's vision as my guiding force – to listen to the voices of the poor and pursue justice over all else. The Jesuits have a long history of men prepared to die for their principles. Not all of the sacrifices they were called on to suffer were imposed from outside the Order. There have been many expelled Jesuits, men who were treated with suspicion and fear and loathing by their fellow clergy and superiors. Knowing this didn't make the challenge of continuing any easier – times *were* hard and the struggle for survival often seemed bleak and hopeless. But there was a great spur to persevere in the stories of men who had suffered for the faith they refused to deny. Men like Alfred Delp, the Jesuit philosopher killed by the Nazis in 1945. Delp once said:

No hopelessness or lack of prospect of success dispenses a person from saying what they have to say. Once you start thinking about the success or efficacy of your decision, then you are lost.

Quoted in *The Jesuit Mystique*, Douglas Letson and Michael Higgins,

Fount Paperbacks, 1996

Thinking about these words for a few minutes, thinking of the man himself and what happened to him, was a considerable help in pushing back any encroaching despondency. Was I scared? Well, the only answer I can give is that, even though during most of the time I was on the island I felt I was on the edge of a precipice, maybe I didn't properly understand what to be scared is. I had a simple philosophy, one which I kept repeating to myself: as long as I can keep going, I will.

Nevertheless, I was getting more and more intimations that the Bishop of Raphoe, the Parish Priest of Gortahork and various other clergy of the diocese – and my own Provincial – were seriously displeased about what I was saying and doing. No one ever categorically told me that I had to leave, that I was on the wrong tack, never told me 'Stop!'; but I was made to feel their displeasure by the manner in which I was slowly and systematically marginalized.

By mid 1981 I had still not been paid the money that Bishop MacFeely agreed would be handed over by the Parish Priest of Gortahork, Fr McGlynn. I actually wondered if a deliberate policy was being carried out to make me so uncomfortable that I'd virtually be starved out.

The problems over food became so acute that I had to resort to the good offices and charitable instincts of a Jesuit lay brother in Dublin, who gave me a black plastic bin liner filled with food each time I managed to come to the capital. I was both extremely grateful and extremely embarrassed. The embarrassment was exacerbated by having to smuggle the bag into *teach sagairt* each time I returned to the island. I couldn't tell Mary McGinley, or any of the other islanders, of my excruciating situation. If Mary came across the food in the refrigerator, and thought I had bought supplies on the mainland – all well and good. If she had her suspicions, she never mentioned them.

The Jesuit Provincial, the Very Rev. Joseph Dargan SJ, inevitably got to know about the failure of the Diocese of Raphoe to pay me what I was due, and I was urged to meet with Bishop MacFeely. When I met the bishop, he listened patiently, said he would 'see about it' and wrote me a cheque for £100 – 'to tide you over for the time being.' From then on, small amounts of money filtered through – but only when I wrote or telephoned as a reminder. It was a humiliating experience which got worse as time wore on. Individuals in positions of responsibility in the Church who knew the predicament I was in, who knew about the injustice and about the personal hardship the injustice caused me, did next to nothing to help.

When Bishop MacFeely's time as Bishop of Raphoe ended and he was succeeded by Bishop Seamus Hegarty in March 1982, I repeatedly informed the new bishop that I was not being paid my wages. I telephoned the residence and sent letters and bank statements. Bishop Hegarty didn't dispute it; indeed, he promised me that I would be paid the money I was due. Unfortunately, the money only came through at long intervals, and wasn't helped by the fact that Fr McGlynn and I hadn't been on the best of terms. On one occasion, we'd had a heated exchange when Fr McGlynn upbraided me for speaking publicly on behalf of the Tory islanders, and criticized me for drawing such media attention to Tory.

The following month, I decided I'd have to visit Bishop Seamus Hegarty personally at the Palace in Letterkenny, to talk directly to him about my work and the fact that I was not receiving what I saw as essential support. I'd not received any public declaration of support from him, which I was unhappy about. But I didn't want to have a view of him that was distorted or one-sided; it was essential that I meet him and get to know him properly.

We began by chatting about Tory's inaccessibility; I mentioned that the crossing, particularly in winter, was often hazardous. He said his colleagues had told him as much, and I was immediately reminded of some islanders' complaints that he hadn't visited them yet. He went on to acknowledge receiving my letters to him about not being paid, as well as some copies of press cuttings. He said he had written back to me, but I hadn't received his letter.

He told me that I'd done 'enormous work' on the island, setting about 'with enthusiasm and determination' to draw the attention of the public on a national basis to Tory, in a way that hadn't been done before. I, in turn, felt that I could be quite open with him, and I told him that I didn't feel I had the backing of the hierarchy. The bishop didn't refute or deny that. Instead, he professed himself 'extremely grateful' for my work on Tory Island.

However, he then went on to indicate reservations he had about my methods of campaigning. Whereas he would favour a somewhat more cautious approach, he felt I perhaps was being too forceful. I asked him for an example, and he referred directly to reports and accounts in the press that I was hitting the County Council 'very hard'. I agreed! I explained how there had been *uisce fé thalamh* (literally, 'water under the ground', i.e. hidden agendas), and described how I had tried to obtain official information on the matter from the Council; how it was very difficult to get it, and that since it was an emergency that needed to be tackled, sometimes I had to adopt a forceful manner if I was to get anything done. I described what the islanders were going through, and how I felt I had to help them, even when there were many obstacles in my path.

The bishop went on to describe his experiences in dealing with such matters, matters between Church and State. He suggested that people were more likely to help if you approached them in a timid way, to avoid offending anyone's sensibilities. I had to stand my ground. I described to him the instance when I had approached a priest on the mainland and asked for facilities to say Mass. That priest actually told me that I was wasting my time and my energies bothering about such a small number of people, and that I'd be far better off ministering to people on the mainland because 'there are thousands of them'. How could I ignore comments such as these?

The bishop listened to all I said in silence. Then, looking down, he said 'You are alleged to have made a comment – whether it was fact or imaginary, I don't know – that you were the only priest who tried to improve the lot of the Tory people.' He raised his eyes and looked at me, waiting for my answer.

I told him I had *never* said any such thing, and never would.

'Or words to that effect?' he pressed.

'No,' I said, 'Never.'

'Let me finish, let me finish,' he continued. 'I know that former priests, curates of Tory, took very grave exception to that.'

I said I was sure they would have done, so went on to explain where I thought such a rumour could have come from. It was at the prize-giving function when our drama group took first prize. A certain priest of the diocese, intoxicated and foul-mouthed, had come up to me. He said aggressively, 'Do you think that you're the only one who ever did anything for Tory?' A heated debate had followed in which I defended my actions, whilst acknowledging that all former priests would have provided the necessary *spiritual* care that the islanders needed. Maybe all that I did differently was to harness the media to our cause, get the islanders motivated to *fight*, and be forthright in standing up for their rights.

'Whatever the circumstances,' the bishop finally replied, 'I don't know and I don't *wish* to know…'

The comment affected me deeply. I left the meeting feeling that perhaps the bishop didn't believe me, that maybe he believed the accusations made against me by other clergy. It didn't augur well for the future.

In June 1982, I decided to write to a number of bishops about the Tory situation. I never knew whether the Irish Catholic hierarchy developed any positive interest in Tory Island or its inhabitants, since no bishop ever spoke to me about the place apart from when I decided to go there, and when I finally returned to the mainland. I felt it was time to do something new.

So I wrote to five bishops on the western seaboard who had islands within their dioceses; namely, of Cork and Ross, Kerry, Galway, Tuam and Raphoe. Some friends told me I was wasting my time, but I was naive enough to think that at least one of the bishops would write back to me. This was the text of the letter:

Dear Bishop,

You know already that Tory Island has a grave problem. We have now reached a crucial point, and so we are trying to lobby support to save the island. I think you know that there are many factors contributing to the present tragic situation, and one very important one is the Church itself.

The Diocese of Raphoe has apparently lost interest and would prefer to see the place closed down. What other conclusion can you come to when you know about the reluctance of the local priests, who used to stay on the island for no more than six months and then depart? It was the perfect recipe for disintegration, and collapse would have taken place this year if it wasn't for the tremendous

*fightback by the Co-op and the community and myself, since I
came here in 1980 on an open-ended invitation.*

*Please write to the County Manager, Donegal County Council,
Lifford, asking him to develop Tory, not close it, expressing your
concern and solidarity for the Tory islanders who want to stay and
develop the place.*

A letter to the Taoiseach *would be a great help. A letter to the
Cardinal, Tomás O Fíach, would probably open the door to Tory
being discussed at the June meeting of the Bishops in Maynooth. A
press statement of solidarity with the islanders would be a tremendous boost to obtain minimum demands. The next couple of
months is vital for Tory. In fact, its fate will probably be decided by
then. That indicates the dire situation we are in just now. Please
don't hesitate to support this worthy cause. If Tory goes this year, it
can't ever be recovered.*

Slán agus beannacht Dé leat *(Health and God's blessing to you)*

I heard nothing. Not one of the five bishops even bothered to acknowledge my letter. When I told the islanders they weren't the
slightest surprised. They knew I'd hear nothing; they knew the
score. I realized that even after all this time, I was still learning it.
I felt let down. Maybe, I thought ruefully, if I'd made an appeal
on behalf of the island's donkeys, dogs, chickens, hens or
seabirds, I'd have had a better chance of a response. I might just
as well have scribbled a note, set fire to it, and sent it up the chimney like a child's letter to Father Christmas.

So why hadn't anyone bothered to reply? Maybe they'd pushed
island people further down their lists of priorities. Maybe they
didn't like people who rocked their boat, especially a priest of
my age!

All I knew could be summed up in the words of the Rome
Synod of 1971: 'The Church's mission involves defending and

promoting the dignity and fundamental rights of the human person.' Even if these words were sometimes forgotten or ignored, it didn't mean that the duties implied by their declaration should be abandoned. Trying to bring help and comfort to people in the distress brought about by poverty (whatever the form of their poverty) should always be a primary, worthwhile duty.

I could therefore never agree with those who held that the solution for the people of Tory Island was to try to integrate them into the structure of mainland culture. The battle on their behalf was based on their rights to dignity and self-esteem – fundamental human rights which no State or Church should attempt to take away.

I was to be further shocked by the encounter I had soon after with Fr McGlynn, who came over to the island to see me. He was in an extremely confrontational mood; and when I switched on a cassette recorder it didn't exactly appease the situation. I was determined to keep whatever was said on record.

'If you say any more,' I said, 'it'll be on record to be reported.'

'Go to the bishop!' he told me.

'If we are both priests, surely we can act rationally?' I replied.

'You're not acting as a priest – you won't even call on your Parish Priest!'

'Surely you can begin to *act* as one, at least *sometimes*. There doesn't seem to be any reason for this to continue.'

'Get on the TV again, get on the radio, and run the island down into the ground,' he taunted.

'You'll have your time to answer it.'

'I've done enough talk!'

'You *haven't*! You haven't opened your mouth on it. You are afraid to face them!'

If that reads ugly, it's because it *was* ugly. He reiterated what I'd heard many say before, that priests aren't social workers and that other priests working on the island had not neglected it, despite what I may have thought. I stood my ground. I knew I had to speak out and take a lead, even if others didn't.

A great opportunity came in December 1982, in the shape of an article published in the Irish language magazine, *An t-Ultach*. The piece was called '*Tóraigh – Bás no Beatha*' – 'Tory – Death or Life', and it included an interview I gave Micheál Ó Máirtín, the editor, published in a 'question and answer' format.

I answered his questions with my usual frankness, held back nothing, said what I felt, told him what I had discovered and what I believed needed to be done. I spoke of the neglect that had been perpetrated, the hopes and aspirations of the islanders, the disappointments they had suffered. I talked about how the school was in need of repair; that there were no catering facilities on the island for tourists who might wish to visit; that there were very few places which could accommodate overnight visitors; that we needed a harbour and an airstrip – basically, all manner of basic facilities.

I spoke of my anger at the treatment meted out to the islanders, my anger at the contemptuous drip-feeding of shameful little amounts of money, and how it seemed to us that the authorities just wanted to let the island die. I mentioned the fact that some is-landers had already left the island, to live in Falcarragh, but that some were already returning; although they had houses, they had-n't got work. All the islanders wanted, I said, was a chance. As it was, they might just as well have been living on another planet. The interview ended with a plea to all readers of *An t-Ultach* to speak out on Tory's behalf, to write to the newspapers. I said it was a cry from the heart. Everything I said was published, unedited.

The magazine was hardly on sale when the editor began to re-ceive angry phone calls from people who identified themselves as priests of the Raphoe diocese. They said the feature was disgraceful, and that its publication by him was an even bigger disgrace. It was, they said, a slap in the face for Bishop Hegarty and themselves. Furthermore, they told him, it was all *ráiméis* – rubbish – and that he, the editor, should be ashamed of himself for running it.

He recounted all this to me on the phone.

'And what did you say?' I asked.

'I told all of them the same thing, that if they cared to send me their views, I'd publish them. I even said that I'd set space aside specially and hold it pending the arrival of their material.'

Perhaps not surprisingly, he never heard from them again. He didn't receive one written line of rebuttal of my views. After all their bluster and blather on the phone about me and what I'd said, and about the magazine and its editor, they walked away; they went to ground. I obviously engendered rage in clerical circles by my outspoken views and actions, yet no one chose to refute my claims when given the opportunity.

The process of marginalization against me continued.

10

WINNIE AND ME AND STRASBOURG

When I picked up the phone that day, I didn't realize quite what a chain of events was going to be set in motion. The caller announced herself as Winifred Ewing – I hadn't a clue who she was, so asked her to explain herself further. It turned out she was an MEP and vigorous campaigner on behalf of the Scottish Highlands and offshore inhabited islands. She had picked up my name from the media, had read all about Tory Island and our campaign to save it. She said that she would be visiting Ireland shortly (June 1983) with a group of MEPs from the European Community's Regional Committee, and asked whether it would be possible to meet up.

'Will you be anywhere near Lifford?' I asked, when I'd finally got over my surprise at hearing from her.

She consulted her diary. 'Yes,' she answered, 'we're due to stop off there for lunch.'

'Right,' I said, 'I'll be there, and with a bit of luck maybe we can get together.'

We decided upon the time and venue, and I made sure I was on time for our appointment. I stood outside the hotel where the

Regional Committee was meeting and waited for her to arrive. As I did, I saw some familiar faces: John Healy (the journalist); John Hume (head of the SDLP party and MEP) and Joe McCartin (MEP), for example. I suddenly realized I didn't even know what Winnie Ewing looked like, and so was thoroughly relieved when an unfamiliar looking woman came striding towards me, stood in front of me, and said: 'Father, how very good to see you – I'm Winnie Ewing.'

She managed to arrange for me to stay for lunch, which was splendid. I also managed to speak to John Hume; I knew he'd spoken well on behalf of Rathlin Island so, ever the opportunist, I filled him in on our cause. He listened in his serious way, but said that since MEPs from the Republic were present, protocol prevented him from becoming too deeply involved.

When the formalities of dinner were over, Winnie and I began to talk in earnest about Tory. John Healy would later say that from where he stood, it was a toss-up as to who won the conversation, that the flush on my face 'was not all Tory sunburn', and that I was 'like a cat who had got a pint of double cream … eyes positively gleaming.' I was bowled over by Winnie's enthusiasm and knowledge; like any good lawyer, she had quickly mastered the brief. She had first-hand knowledge of the island's problems and solutions, its people and their hopes, island rights, cherished tradition and history. In short, she showed sympathy for and empathy with everything I told her about Tory. As she put it, here was an island with a small population that still spoke the Irish language. If we were at all serious about saving the language, we should save Tory.

'The principal thing we must do, Father, is plan. Let's plan.'

This was sweet music to me. 'I'm ready,' I said. 'I'll go along with whatever you suggest, whatever it takes.'

'Good. It's important to do this right,' she affirmed.

'Of *course*,' I said. 'Do it right, and keep it right.'

'We'll hit Dublin first,' she said, 'and if Dublin doesn't answer—'

'It *won't*,' I cut in, 'and it *didn't* – I've been along that road already.'

'Then we'll hit Strasbourg,' Winnie said with tremendous determination.

I had, of course, heard of Strasbourg, and knew that the European Parliament was based there, but I didn't know much about what they actually did. In the early '80s, the European Parliament didn't have much relevance for those of us living outside the mainstream of politics. Therefore, I knew very little about its functions. I had no idea that European co-operation in all fields, except defence, was its principal objective, and that there was a particular stress laid on the safeguarding of human rights, improving the quality of life, and strengthening democratic institutions. Up until now, I had had 'tunnel vision', directing all my political efforts to Tory, the Donegal County Council and the Dublin government. Winnie Ewing's robust declaration had the effect of a bomb being thrown into the tunnel, smashing the sides out, revealing open spaces, pushing horizons back. I understood what she was proposing and instinctively knew that approaching the European Parliament would be an enormously important step for us. It had to be done.

I found Winnie Ewing to be vastly enthusiastic, warm, witty, and as diplomatic as she judged the occasion warranted. Her diplomacy didn't extend, for example, to disguising how singularly unimpressed she was by the quality and performances of the Irish MEPs at Strasbourg, particularly in relation to campaigning on behalf of the islands. And she was right. 'I'll keep in contact,' Winnie assured me at the end of our meeting, 'I'll be in touch.' They were no empty promises.

I was fired up by my meeting with Winnie, and I made an irrevocable decision to tie in with whatever tactics and ploys she might suggest. Then, as so frequently happens, I began to have doubts and questions. Was latching on to her interest and offers of help simply grasping at straws? Should I follow her or would it all be a waste of time? I had to balance these against the knowledge that set-backs in the past had caused introspection and moments of doubt, and that while I had started off with considerable enthusiasm, a positive attitude can – on occasions – be extremely difficult to sustain. It isn't always the person who is most enthusiastic at the beginning who ultimately finishes the job. I wanted to see the Tory job through to the finish. In the end, I decided I would just have to press on.

About a week after our first meeting, I received the promised phone call from Winnie. She told me that she was arranging for me to fly to Strasbourg in October 1983, so that I could mount an exhibition in the European Parliament building about Tory. There, I would be able to show, in a bold, dramatic way, what was happening on the island and how a whole community was in danger of being destroyed. I was ecstatic; I couldn't quite believe that it was happening. Her commitment and vision gave a new impetus to our campaign; it was as if she was providing a beacon on a dark and treacherous coastline. Words from Longfellow's 'The Lighthouse' were particularly apt:

> And as the evening darkens, lo! How bright,
> through the deep purple of the twilight air,
> Beams forth the sudden radiance of its light
> with strange, unearthly splendour in the glare.

Any doubts I had in my mind about working with Winnie were forgotten. The idea was terrific, I was only too happy to be able to spread news of Tory Island and our work to save it. In the Parliament building, Winnie Ewing made her staff available to me to lend a hand. They helped me put up the pictures I had brought, and to lay out pamphlets and leaflets on the tables. Winnie herself had chosen the corridor in this fortress of democracy where Tory's plight would be brought to the attention of the passing politicians. It was up to me to try to ensure that they didn't pass by and ignore us. So I'd taken with me about 500 copies of a little pamphlet we had prepared called, 'A Case of Deliberate Neglect', and made sure that everyone who walked past was given one. The booklet was small enough to slip easily into a jacket pocket or handbag.

I didn't find it easy. It gave me a little insight into what it must be like to be a beggar on the streets when people affect not to notice, looking in the other direction, or focusing on something inconsequential in their hands. But Winnie's choice of location was brilliant. The MEPs had to pass backwards and forwards through this corridor every day. Each time they did, they were confronted by numerous pictures of Tory, a table containing leaflets and other literature, and one slightly bewildered Jesuit priest of advancing years eager to talk to them about the island and its people.

It was exciting. I was being introduced to various frontline politicians from mainland Europe, and was given the opportunity to talk to them directly about Tory. The only politicans who were very familiar with what I was describing were some Germans who had seen the documentary on television. And it was a source of recurring amazement to me (and no little embarrassment) that the efforts and encouragement which should have been coming from one of the 15 Irish MEPs were instead coming from a *Scottish* MEP. John Hume did stop several times at the table to chat, and asked whether he could do anything to help. But I didn't get much of a response from Joe McCartin. At lunchtime one day he began to talk about Tory Island, the exhibition and my presence in Strasbourg in a disparaging, almost 'jokey' manner. I didn't find it amusing, particularly when he suggested that I should have held the exhibition in Buswell's Hotel, a favourite drinking spot for politicians just across the road from the parliament in Dublin. But I refused to let anyone get my spirits down. I would keep on fighting.

Most politicians, however, *had* been genuinely interested in the exhibition – including the Irish MEPs – and signed a motion which Winnie had prepared. The motion asked that the Parliament should accept, as a basic right, that isolated communities such as Tory should have an acceptable level of communications and transportation services. I was disappointed, however, that the Irish MEPs made no further plans to meet and discuss the situation back in Ireland.

All in all, though, it had been a fantastic week, a really worthwhile experience, and I was grateful beyond words to Winnie for her help. All we had to do now was wait and see what would come out of it. On the last day of the exhibition, I sat in a restaurant with Winnie Ewing, John Hume and Seán Flanagan (another Irish MEP) discussing the week's campaign. Suddenly I heard John Hume saying: 'There's the Big Man.' I followed his gaze, and there, standing just inside the door, was Ian Paisley, big, heavy-shouldered, bespectacled, his hair impeccably combed in those familiar straight lines. Dr Paisley, the militant Northern Ireland Protestant clergyman and politician, set up his own Church in 1951 – the Free Presbyterian Church of Ulster. He also founded the Protestant Unionist Party, standing as its MP from 1970 until 1974. Since then, he has been the Democratic Unionist MP for North Antrim and became an MEP in 1970. He is known to be fiercely opposed to Roman Catholicism. I'd seen him several times during the week, but he was always deep in conversation, or concentrating on papers he was reading; for these reasons, and because of our immensely different backgrounds – political as well as religious – I was wary about trying to attract his attention.

John Hume, however, was more decisive. He walked over to Paisley and started talking to him. Paisley's voice boomed out over the clatter of cutlery and plates and cups and saucers, and the chatter of conversation: 'Where is he? I've been looking for him all week!'

Hume led him over to where we sat. When they were standing over us, John nodded towards Winnie and Seán Flanagan and said, 'I think you know these two.'

'Aye, aye.'

'But I don't think you've met Father Ó Péicín before?'

'No, I haven't. How do you do, Father?'

Paisley put out his large hand and shook mine.

'I've been hearing about your campaign. I admire what you've been doing on behalf of those people out there on Tory Island. Look, have you got a minute or two?'

'Yes, certainly, of course I have.'

'I just thought you might come out to the table with me and explain a few things for me.'

We excused ourselves and I accompanied Ian Paisley back to the exhibition. He plied me with questions and listened attentively to my answers. After having looked at the pictures, and taken various leaflets, he signed the motion.

'We have an island off our Northern Ireland coastline in which I'm particularly interested,' he said. 'Rathlin – I'm sure you know it.'

'Indeed, I know it well,' I told him. 'And one day perhaps we'll visit it together.'

'I hope so,' he said, and I knew the way he said it that the Big Man meant it.

Gerry Moriarty, writing in the *Irish Press*, later said that our handshake – between the voluble Protestant clergyman Unionist and the Papist priest from Dublin via Tory – could become known as the ecumenical gesture of the decade.

By the time Friday came around I was not only fatigued, I was also anxious – anxious to get back to Tory. How were the islanders getting on, I wondered, especially now when the evenings were closing in, and the viciousness of winter was again fast approaching. Here was I, forlorn agitator, adrift in the corridors of power. That last night in the Jesuit house where I was staying, I tried to assess what we'd achieved during the week and what I had to do next. I did a lot of praying. I tussled with the words of St Bonaventure: 'Do not become upset or impatient at the defects of others, for it would be foolish if, upon seeing someone falling into a ditch, you should throw yourself into another uselessly.' I tried to apply them to my own situation and my own propensity to become frustrated and angry when confronted with bureaucratic fudging. I found it hard, though; the word 'defects' can encompass so much.

There was still a great deal I felt I had to do. Wasn't it Horace Mann who said 'Be ashamed to die until you have won some victory for humanity'? How, though, could this be understood in comparison with 'Having done all, to stand' (Ephesians 6:13)? How does one know when 'all' has been done? How would I know when to stop? Any workable strategy for attaining peace of mind has to include acceptance of the inevitable. The difficulty comes in attempting to recognize what is the inevitable. After many hours of praying and mental turmoil, I decided to leave my fears and worries in God's hands; he'd know what was right for me to do. Robert Flaherty's description of the Aran islanders' independence as 'the most precious privilege they can win from life' kept me going.

Before I had left Dublin for Strasbourg, I had telephoned the Irish television station (RTE), in the hope that they might give some coverage to the exhibition at the European Parliament, but it seemed no one was interested. Yet the very day after I returned to Dublin I received a phone call from their reporter, Charlie Bird, in Montrose. Someone must have contacted the media with the story; now Bird was on the line, asking me if I'd do an interview with him for that day's evening news. The 'Strasbourg handshake' with Ian Paisley totally changed the situation!

'Charlie,' I said, 'before I went to Strasbourg, I called you people at RTE hoping you'd do something then, and you weren't interested. But now it's a different matter, isn't it? Now *you* want *me* to co-operate, and all because Ian Paisley and I shook hands in Strasbourg. You're some bunch.'

'Ah well, there you go,' he answered, 'That's the way things are. Well, will you do the interview?'

Of course, I agreed, although I was a little nervous – particularly as there was so little time to prepare. I'd never done a live television interview before. I knew the most important thing was to ensure that I spoke clearly and succinctly and that everything *I* wanted to say got across well. Once in the studio, Bird reassured me.

'Don't worry,' he said, 'just be yourself. There's nothing to worry about.'

When it was over he said, 'There you are, I told you there was nothing to worry about. That was great. The story drives itself. Perfect!'

On the flight home from Strasbourg the previous evening I had felt depressed. I didn't know what the week had accomplished in practical terms. Little did I know just how much public awareness had been building up as a result of increased media attention, and by the time that the evening's news had finished, there was cheering in the houses on Tory Island, and our story had transcended parish, diocesan, County Council and national borders.

11

CAMPAIGNING IN AMERICA

It was only when I was back on Tory that I realized how much the Strasbourg week had taken out of me: the unfamiliar surroundings; the ceaseless talking to strangers, hoping to inform, convince them and win their support; the struggle against tiredness; the struggle to remain (at least on the surface) up-beat and optimistic – it all left me feeling drained.

I did what I had so often done in the past when I needed to renew my spirit – I put on an anorak and my brown woollen island hat, and went for a walk. As I left the houses behind, I pulled my collar up, hunched my neck down, and pressed my hands, balled into fists, deep into my pockets to protect them from the skinning wind. I stopped for a moment by a pool of water, and watched the wind disturbing its surface, blowing little ripples to the water's edge where they died among the bent-over scutch grass. I watched black seabirds balancing on drenched rocks, then a lone gull breasting the gusts, looking left and right, making its own private search. I found it to be a reviving experience, slipping my mind into neutral and letting my eyes dwell on whatever they settled on.

I kept on walking until I came to one of my favourite spots. I stood gazing at the incredible rock formations, the deep fissures cut and carved by gale and sea and sun and rain over thousands of years … I felt very small, very insignificant and very humble.

I let my thoughts come and go as they chose, not attempting to impose a sequence or order of any kind. I thought of how I had spent the £350 gift of the Dublin Lions to buy a welding machine for Tory, and the sense of achievement I had felt when I watched the islanders making 500 tubular steel chairs in their first factory. I thought of the old boat *Marino* which lay in Killybegs and which I had hired for £1,000 – we had used it as a ferry during the *Seachtain Mhór*, charging £5 return fare, and went on to make a £2,000 profit from the purchase.

After a short spell of letting my thoughts freewheel in this way, I felt a lot better, so turned and started to walk back towards the houses. In the distance, three men in patterned ganseys, one of them wearing a blue knitted bobble hat, were leaving a white half-decker on which they had been working. A long-tailed collie bounced expectantly around the feet of one of the men. By the time I reached the boat, all three had disappeared, and I called in to see Pádraig.

'You got back from Europe safe and sound then, Father?' he said. '*Tar isteach agus fáilte rómhat*' – 'Come inside, you're welcome.'

'I'm not stopping a minute, Pádraig,' I said, 'I just dropped in to ask you if you'd round up the other members of the Co-op and come to *teach sagairt* this evening after tea and I'll fill you in on what happened.'

He said, 'Sure didn't we see you on the news and read about you in the paper? You and Paisley! That was some stroke!'

'I'll tell you all about it later, and I have something else to tell you as well.'

The 'something else' I had to tell them related to a small slip of paper in my pocket. Towards the end of the Strasbourg visit, I fell into conversation with a correspondent based there, who plied me with a lot of questions, and listened avidly to what I had to say. He seemed genuinely to want to know the background to my visit, and questioned me closely as to how I felt the exhibition had gone. Had coming to the hub of European politics achieved anything positive? I told him I didn't know. I said that with the year drawing to a close, the storms would soon lock the people of Tory Island into their dark winter isolation again.

'Even if coming over here turns out to have been a waste of time,' I told him, 'I can't afford to think that that would be the end of the road. I don't know what the hell I'm doing after this, but I'll think of *something*.'

'Like what?' he asked.

I was stumped. 'I'm not sure,' I said, 'but I may have to hit America.'

'America?' he echoed incredulously.

'Yes,' I said. 'Do you know there are an estimated forty million Americans with Irish connections?'

'I didn't know that,' he said, 'it seems to be an awful lot, given the size of Ireland.'

'Well, that's what they say anyway,' I said.

I became aware of the stillness of his head and what looked like disbelief on his face, and I stopped. I was embarrassed.

'Forgive me!' I said. 'You must think I'm mad with all this waffle. I'm sorry for going on.'

'Not at all, not at all,' he said. 'Look, I think you *should* go, and if you'd allow me, I'd like to help.'

He reached into his inside pocket and took out a chequebook, and there and then wrote out a cheque for an amount substantial enough to cover my transatlantic fares, and internal travel throughout the United States.

I was dumbfounded, but he waved away my gratitude saying, 'No, I'm pleased to be in a position to be able to do this.' Then he reached for my hand, shook it, and said, 'I wish you great good luck in America, Father. *Bon voyage!*' And he walked away without turning back.

The little group from the Co-op listened to this in silence, some of them with their mouths open. When I finished, Pádraig was the first to speak.

'By God, that's some story!' he gasped. 'We could write a drama around that!'

'And are you really going to go, Father?' asked Jimmy, ever the realist.

'I am,' I said. 'I've made up my mind – I'll head off sometime next year.'

I had never been to America before, and it was with some trepidation that I booked my flight to New York for April 1984, with a return flight 30 days later.

I had only the vaguest, jumbled ideas about a schedule or itinerary, but I contacted Fr Joseph O'Hare, President of Fordham, the Jesuit University in New York State, and asked if he could put me up. I got an immediate 'Yes', a sign of positive co-operation that was to be repeated all over the USA when I sought help from the Society of Jesus.

At Fordham, I was quickly taken to meet Fr O'Hare. As soon as the formality of greetings was over, he said, 'Sit down now and let's talk for half an hour or so – or, rather, you talk to me so that I can try to get a clear picture.'

I filled him in on as much of the background as I could, but I must have gone off on too many tangents because he held up his hand and interrupted me, saying, 'It's chaotic! Hold on a second!'

He picked up a phone, punched in a number, and spoke rapidly: 'This is Father O'Hare. I have Father Ó Péicín here in the office with me. He's over from Ireland and he needs some help. Can you see him right away?'

In this way he immediately put me in touch with the Jesuit communications centre at the university, where I was looked after for a couple of days, with interviews and publicity organized for me. I had barely arrived there when they put me on the air on their own radio station, and started organizing another broadcast for the following day. The staff worked with me on a press release, which was photocopied and distributed in huge quantities. I didn't have any plans worked out, other than hoping to visit various cities with my exhibition of Tory Island. I was given a list of contact addresses and telephone numbers which proved enormously useful.

In due course, I flew up to Boston with my suitcase and the collection of plastic bags in which I transported the materials for the exhibition. At Boston College (a Jesuit college) I got the 'red carpet' treatment, as if I were a VIP; I was quite embarrassed by such unusual conduct! The people there even arranged for the exhibition to be mounted at the city's revered State House. What a start! An invitation was given to me to speak in Boston's House of Representatives, which I was honoured to do. I was presented with a beautiful citation afterwards, which marked my visit and praised my efforts on behalf of Tory.

After such a wonderful start to my tour, I was naturally disappointed to find that some people in the Irish diplomatic service were somewhat unenthused by what I was publicizing, and the manner in which I was conducting my campaign. Patrick Curran, the Irish Consul General, made it apparent to me that he, and those above him – 'official Ireland', if you like – were not happy about the exhibition, reiterating that no money was available for any island improvements. He cited the recent statement (February 1984) by Pádraig Ó Tuathail (the incumbent *Gaelteacht* minister), which outlined that government aid to help Tory Island was unlikely to be granted in the near future, and that since some families had already left the island, he could not be hopeful of providing the facilities we sought. The long hand of resentment was capable of extending across the Atlantic Ocean. But I knew I had to keep battling on – after all, I was in the land of the free.

It was the Rector of Boston College who set me thinking that my visit to America could actually include meeting various politicians. The first one that he suggested was Senator Teddy Kennedy.

'You know how the Kennedys love Ireland,' he said. 'It might do you no harm at all, and a lot of good, to try and get them interested in your Tory Island project.'

It was a great suggestion. Teddy Kennedy could prove a powerful ally in winning the interest and support of the Irish/Americans to help end the discrimination against the Tory islanders. Maybe it would even do him a bit of good among his voters. I worked out what I wanted to say about Tory, the Jesuits' views on justice, and the key point about the dignity of the human person, and started trying to arrange a meeting with him in Washington. I managed to make a provisional date, although it was contingent upon his not being unexpectedly called away on other business.

With my confidence rising, I thought I might as well go for broke, and therefore called the office of the House Speaker, Tip O'Neill. He, too, was one of those powerful American political figures who repeatedly asserted his love for Ireland. He had strong connections with Co. Donegal, owning a farm in the village of Buncrana. This time I wasn't so fortunate. I was told that Mr O'Neill had a full schedule, and might not even be in Washington when I was there. It seemed to me that this was a classic case of a busy and important man being shielded from the plethora of eccentrics, cranks and malcontents who habitually beat paths to such men's doors. I understood the situation, but I hadn't travelled over 2,000 miles to be fobbed off lightly. I said I'd call at the office anyway on the day I was scheduled to be in Washington.

'I doubt very much that it'll do any good, Father,' I was told, 'but you can come visit us if you like.'

'I'll do that,' I said firmly.

When I contacted Teddy Kennedy's office on my arrival in Washington, I learned, sadly, that the Senator had had to leave the city on important business, so I decided to go to Tip O'Neill's office on the off-chance that I might see him. Although I was told that it was 'extremely unlikely' I'd get to see the Speaker – 'he only returned from Africa last night, and he may not even come in to the office today' – I decided to wait and see what happened.

I must have been an object of some curiosity to the staff, sitting there hour after hour, but after a while they got used to me. I used part of the time to dip into my breviary and pray; then I thought about my trip, scarcely believing that I was actually here in Washington. There was an air of unreality about it: here I was in a land of more than 250 million people, trying to interest the Speaker, Tip O'Neill – and anyone else who would listen – in a wild chunk of rock in the sea 2,000 miles away. But it was precisely that rock, where a small, marginalized and voiceless community lived, that stopped me from getting up and leaving the office. I recalled Jerome Nadal's words about the central charism of the Jesuits: 'The Society cares for those persons who are either totally neglected, or inadequately attended to...' Stop thinking 'insignificance', I told myself, you have every right to be here, you have a *responsibility* to *try*.

Many hours after I had first presented myself at Tip O'Neill's office, the door opened and he walked in. He must have caught sight of my Roman collar immediately because, even before my name was announced to him, he strode across to me, right hand outstretched, left hand poised to rest on my shoulder, and said: 'Father!'

'This is Father Ó Péicín from Ireland,' he was informed, and he led me straight into his inner office.

The moment I entered the room I spotted a familiar painting on the wall. I pointed to it and said 'Buncrana.'

'*God*, that was quick!' he said. 'You recognize it?'

'Why wouldn't I?' I said, smiling. 'It's in County Donegal!'

'You know the county well?'

'It's where I work,' I said, 'and that's why I was hoping to see you, to tell you about a place you should know about – Tory Island.'

'Tell me,' he said. And I did.

Several times he shook his head and made sounds of disapproval. When I had finished he said, 'Do you want me to write to your *Taoiseach*, Garret Fitzgerald?'

'Anything,' I said, 'anything at all you'd do would undoubtedly help.'

He scribbled something on a yellow pad on his desk. We continued talking for half an hour or so before an assistant came in to remind him of an appointment that was imminent. Again there was the warm handshake, the hand on the shoulder, the sincerity, the assurances of his interest, and his promise to write to Garret Fitzgerald. And then it was over.

As I left the office, the staff members who had come and gone about their business during my long wait, all smiled and wished me luck. I felt great. I felt very optimistic. O'Neill could be a powerful ally, and the seeds of interest had been sown in him. The next time I came back, things would be on a different footing.

Next stop, New York. There, I contacted Paddy Reilly, an Irishman at whose brother's marriage ceremony I had officiated in London. 'You're here on the ground, and you know your way around – I know *no one*,' I said to him. 'Will you gather as much information as you can lay your hands on about Irish associations and clubs in the area? It would be very handy for me.'

He said he'd start work on it straight away. A few days later he got in touch with me again and reported good progress, and said that he'd have a list ready for me very soon.

'By the way,' he added, 'there's a meeting of the IAUC on tonight in the Engineers' Hall, and Jim Delaney'll be there. You should try to get along and see if you can talk to him.'

'What's the IAUC?' I asked, 'and who is Jim Delaney?'

'The Irish American Unity Conference,' he answered. 'Have you never heard of them?'

'No, I haven't,' I said. 'You may have forgotten that I've been "buried" out on Tory Island for the past few years; lots of things happen in the world which we never get to hear about out there. Now, who is Jim Delaney?'

'He's the founder of the IAUC; his idea was to unify the many Irish organizations in the States and form a cohesive political lobby. He's also a millionaire – probably a *billionaire*, he's really important round here.'

'Right,' I said with a laugh, 'lead me to him.'

I found out some more details about Delaney before the meeting that evening. Delaney was a former basketball star and Golden Gloves boxer, who had become a marine and then gone to College. He had earned himself a degree in philosophy, and subsequently made a fortune as a successful businessman. He was a blunt, straight-talking Irish American.

The death in Northern Ireland of 12-year-old Carol Ann Kelly, killed by a plastic bullet fired by a member of the security forces, had enraged him. He had a daughter the same age, and news of the tragedy affected him deeply. He decided to post a plastic bul-let, similar to that which had ended Carol Ann Kelly's life, to every member of Congress. Each bullet would be accompanied by a letter setting out the names of the children killed by these weapons in Northern Ireland. The communication also pointed out that although the use of plastic bullets had been officially condemned by the European Parliament, and the British had out-lawed their use in England, Wales and Scotland, similar condi-tions had not been imposed on Northern Ireland. After learning all this, I couldn't wait to meet him.

When I arrived at the Engineers' Hall, the meeting was nearly over. I chatted with the doorman until the people started to drift out, and then went in to meet Delaney. He towered over me, bent down to catch what I was saying, and took me aside so that we could talk uninterruptedly for a few minutes. He had that brusqueness, with intimations of impatience, which together seem part of many successful businessmen's make-up.

'So what are you doing over here?' he asked. 'And why did you want to tell me all this?'

'I'm over here to rustle up some support,' I said. 'I'm over here to publicize a scandal. And I was given to understand that since you are said to be so interested in Ireland, you might be worth speaking to. But if you're not interested, I'm sorry for wasting your time – and for wasting my own as well.'

'Now, now, Father, no need to get on your high horse –'

'I'm not getting on any high horse at all,' I cut in. 'You asked me, and I told you.'

'Is it money you want?' he asked.

'No,' I said. 'I didn't come to you with a begging bowl. I didn't come to America with a begging bowl. I came to highlight something awful, something that people should know about so that, if they're interested, they can show some solidarity with the people of Tory Island. I came to plant some seeds of thought, to make people think. That's all. Then, *if* they think about it and want to *do* something, maybe if I come back later in the year we might be able to mobilize some support, economic or otherwise.'

He visibly softened, and we left each other on the best of terms, he promising to give Tory Island and its people 'a lot of thought', and I thanking him for his time and saying I'd get back to him if and when I made a return visit to America.

I met with various Donegal Association branches and groups, gave talks, answered questions and asked them to set up branches of *Cáirde Thórai*, Friends of Tory, wherever and whenever they could. For the most part, the reception I received was enthusiastic, warm and supportive.

My 30-day trip encompassed New York, Boston, Washington, Joliet (Illinois), San Francisco and Los Angeles. I appeared on talk shows and gave numerous newspaper interviews. One particularly successful one was with the *San Francisco Chronicle* – they talked about the 'diabolical, despicable plot' which I was 'shouting and howling from Strasbourg to Dublin to New York to San Francisco'; they even tried to contact Selma Doran, the Irish Consul General in San Francisco, but she refused to discuss Tory and its plight.

It had been an extraordinary 30 days, flying from city to city. I thanked as many of the wonderfully warm and co-operative people as I could, who had helped me every mile of the way – including the Boston ladies who, seeing the disreputable-looking collection of plastic bags in which I carried the exhibition materials, had said 'Oh my goodness – they're *awful*!' and proceeded to buy me a splendid leather carrier!

I thought about all of them as the plane taxied out from the terminal at Kennedy Airport. I looked at the darkening evening sky and the first, faint, blinking stars. The long journey home awaited me. I had one last, long flight over the night-covered ocean to Shannon and Dublin, then the drive north-west to Magheraroarty, and finally the sea trip in a half-decker out to Tory to come.

I was winding down. I didn't wish to talk to my fellow passengers in the seats on each side of me, so I put my head back and closed my eyes. Presently I slept.

In hardly any time at all, it seemed, I was back in Ireland and on my way back to Tory. When the half-decker eased away from Magheraroarty pier and headed for the open sea and the island, I experienced the familiar surge of anticipation. I sat alone in the bow, facing sternwards at first, looking at the mainland, at the imposing mountains shouldering the sky, providing such a magnificent backdrop.

Presently, when I was covered in cold seaspray from a wave onto which the bow slapped, I turned and faced Tory. This was a world so utterly different from international airports, interstate highways, screaming police cars hurtling along canyon-like streets, thrusting, impatient crowds, alien accents and bad-tempered drivers at the wheels of clapped-out, frayed-seated taxis – I just opened my mouth and gulped in lungfuls of the freshening wind coming in from the Atlantic. I was home again.

12

SHATTERED!

Everyone wanted to know all about the American trip, and I told them as much as I could remember.

'And the Jesuits were good to you, Father, were they?' asked Pádraig.

'They couldn't have been better, nothing was too much trouble for them.'

'And you told them all about us at that State House in Boston?' Jimmy asked.

'I told them everything, all of them, everywhere I went.'

'And that Tip O'Neill man, did he listen? Will he help us d'you think? Sure hasn't he some class of a farm in the county?' pressed Jimmy.

'Oh, he listened all right, and as for will he help, only time will tell.'

Pádraig came straight to the point.

'Will anything definite come out of that month you spent beyond?' he asked. 'Anything of a positive nature?'

'Pádraig,' I said, 'I can't tell what the future holds, no more than you can. By and large, though, many more people know about us now than did before I went. I'm looking on the American trip as a ground-preparing exercise. The people over there were given a lot to think about, and I came away with the feeling that when I go back – if I go back – there'll be a massive amount of goodwill and support waiting to be picked up.'

'On behalf of all of us, Father, *go raibh míle maith agat* – a thousand thanks,' Pádraig said. 'Now you must be jaded tired. Why don't you try and get some rest?'

It was only a few months later in July 1984 that my 'rest' was over. The phone rang one morning in *teach sagairt*. When I answered it, a man's voice said dispassionately, 'Your replacement from next Sunday will be Father Kerr.' Then the caller hung up.

I stood for a moment, the phone in my hand. Then, suddenly, I felt my legs becoming weak and my stomach sick. I stumbled and sat down. I don't know how long I was there, not moving at first, not wanting to. I remember putting my hand to my mouth and holding it there, breathing noisily through the fingers.

After a while I stood up and searched through my papers until I found what I was looking for – Bishop MacFeely's letter which he had typed on 7 August 1980. I read and re-read the second paragraph, the one containing his welcome to me 'to act as curate for as long as he wishes on Tory Island...'

'*for as long as he wishes...*'

Now it was all over, and the ending had nothing at all to do with *my* wishes.

I called a meeting of the Co-op and gave them the news, just as it had been given to me, unembellished, brutal in its brevity. I don't know who it was, but one of them said: 'Ignore it, Father! *Stay!*'

There was silence for a moment, and suddenly Pádraig erupted into loud anger. He swore savagely, and ended by saying, 'This can't be happening!'

'I'm afraid it is, Pádraig,' I said. 'If the bishop decides that I have to move on, then I have to go.'

'Well, he'll have to answer to us. I'll send him a wire and I'll tell him he'd better come here and do some explaining.' Then, looking abject and helpless, he asked, 'What'll we do without you?'

I touched the back of his hand, and even with that small action I nearly broke down.

'You'll get by,' I said. They'd have to.

I decided that I'd say Mass that afternoon at 3 o'clock. Very early in the Mass, when I looked at the faces of the congregation, many of them showing the glistening tracks of tears on their cheeks, I broke down completely and cried. It was terrible. I could hear the sounds of grief, theirs and mine. I didn't think I could complete the Mass. I thought I wouldn't be able to get through to the end.

After Mass, I returned to my house to pack up my belongings. I stuffed the few things I'd accumulated – the woolly island hat, books – together with my clothes and breviary into a couple of black plastic bags. The letters, documents, and other papers which I might need in the future, I put into cardboard boxes.

A few days later, when the time came finally to leave, I looked around *teach sagairt* for the last time. I found myself looking at mundane and familiar things – the fireplace, chairs, a table. Time, for a few minutes, seemed to be suspended. I don't think I really believed I was leaving. After a while, I shook my head vigorously and took some deep breaths in a conscious effort to get back to reality. Training, instinct and years of practice – as well as a lifelong conviction – prompted me to pray. I cried out to God, shattered, desperate, in need of help.

I was skewered by fear and rage: fear for myself, fear of becoming bitter; fear, too, for the islanders; fear for what might become of them if the continuous fight and effort in which I had been involved wasn't carried on. My rage stemmed from the feeling that I'd tried to destroy a cancer and failed. I had struggled and kicked against the oppression visited upon these splendid people, to no avail. It had been imperative to fight those who so arrogantly felt they had the right to decide the islanders' future for them. To have done nothing would have been a betrayal. As a result, I had been characterized as a dissident priest, agitator priest – all because I had answered that call so clear in the words and life of Christ, to fight against injustice of every kind.

Eventually it was time to go down to the pier to the waiting boat. Some of the people who came to the front door to see if I needed any assistance gathered up my belongings and went on ahead of me. I looked back at St Colmcille's, so dear to me, and had to force myself to turn away and keep walking towards the pier, where Rosie Rodgers had greeted me on my first visit to Tory. I glanced at the Tau cross, and made my way down the slope to the pier, past the waiting knot of people standing there. Some of them reached out and touched my hand, others just stood still, shaking their heads, or keeping their eyes down cast. Pádraig, moist-eyed, tried to act defiant, and failed. Jimmy grabbed my hand with his strong fisherman's fingers and pressed hard. I couldn't trust myself to speak.

Someone, I don't know who, gave me a helping hand to board the boat which then cast off and began to back out from the pier before making the wide sweeping turn which would face the bow towards Muckish Mountain and Errigal Mountain. I waved feebly a few times at the figures on the pier, but I couldn't really distinguish their faces. I turned towards the bow which was beginning to dip into the long, easy swell. Bloody Foreland and Horn Head were clearly visible, but not to me. I kept my eyes closed until we went alongside at Magheraroarty.

My car awaited me; relieved when it started at the first turn of the ignition key, I drove away as fast as I could. I went south through Crolly, Loughanure, Dungloe and Maas, where I turned towards the west for a few miles, eventually swinging south through Kilclooney.

My mind jumped and hopped and skittered over a confusing profusion of thoughts and images, snippets of half-remembered talk, facial expressions, small triumphs, disasters, things done and things left undone. Phrases from Scripture came to mind: 'I will not leave you comfortless; I will come to you' (John 14:18); 'Thou wilt keep him in perfect peace whose mind is stayed on thee' (Isaiah 26:3); 'Trust in the Lord with all thine heart; and lean not unto thine own understanding. In all thy ways acknowledge him, and he shall direct thy paths' (Proverbs 3:5–6). I was almost shouting that last sentence, forcing it home: '… and he shall direct thy paths.' I certainly hoped so.

I drove as though operating on some kind of auto-pilot. I wasn't aware of searching out signposts to ensure I was on the correct route. But I arrived safely – at the house of John Molloy, the friend who had supported me so strongly over the years, and who'd helped us set up the knitting factory. I had taken to calling periodically to the Molloys' house during my many trips to the mainland. It was a place where I could unwind; they were hospitable, warm people I grew to admire and appreciate, people with whom I could just be myself.

'There's always a room for you in our house, Father,' he and his wife had said more than once. 'We're always here for you.' And they were. They were the first people I thought to turn to on the day I left Tory Island. I felt bruised and fragile when I went to their front door, but I knew that if I made a cry of pain, it would be understood and not questioned. Though I'd come unannounced, I knew they'd be happy to see me.

'Father! Welcome! Come in! *Failte romhat*,' said John on opening the door.

I stood there for a moment, wordless, helpless, feeling suddenly tired and utterly drained, feeling – for the first time – old.

'Come on in,' he said, putting his arm around my shoulder, 'your room is waiting for you.'

As I expected, John and his wife were sympathetic and supportive. Priests were always welcomed at their house; indeed, a day or two after I arrived, I was sitting in my room thinking, when there was a knock at the front door. It was opened by Mrs Molloy, and I heard a man's voice greeting her, then the sound of footsteps as the pair of them walked into the hall. Presently she knocked on my door. She came in and told me that it was the local priest. 'He often drops in,' she said. 'He's a nice man, and I know he's sympathetic to you, but you don't have to come out and meet him if you'd prefer not to. I haven't mentioned that you are here. What do you think?'

I didn't particularly want to see or talk to anyone at that stage, but at the same time I didn't want to be awkward or appear to be running away, so I decided I might as well say a quick 'Hello'. I'm glad I did. What a difference to be in conversation with someone who asked no inquisitorial questions, nor flattered nor made unbecoming attacks, nor went in for name-calling or labelling of anyone. I was thankful for that.

My time at the Molloys' was ideal for reflection, a chance to stand back from it all, to try to realize what had happened and why.

Over the next few days, various people commented on my departure. The Bishop of Raphoe denied that the Church and State wanted to evacuate the island. He said that my transfer was a routine diocesan change, and I was being replaced by a priest who'd served on the island in 1978. 'It is my policy to change priests more frequently than usual,' he added.

Charles Haughey, when contacted for his views, said he understood the bishop's authority in moving priests within a diocese, but said that 'it would be a great pity if, for diocesan reasons, Fr Ó Péicín would not be able to continue his work for Tory.' Importantly, he told me personally that he'd received a phone call from Bishop Hegarty himself, upbraiding him strongly for standing up for me. He got a real 'belt of the crozier' that day, but he didn't lay down meekly under attack. That was never his style.

Gerry Moriarty of the *Irish Press* was outspoken in his comments:

> Now that he has got the Episcopal red card, islanders fear that what was achieved, and what was promised, will be lost … the events of the past ten days have cemented the view that the authorities would prefer to see Tory a 'deserted rock' – the islanders don't accept that the transfer of their outspoken curate … was a simple diocesan move … Whether even a Jesuit can succeed against the power of the crozier is a moot point. In the meantime, the islanders feel they are rudderless because they do not feel they have got the confidence in themselves to take on the authorities in their campaign for better conditions.

After a couple of days spent trying to pull myself out of the emotional quagmire, I thought I'd better leave the Molloys in peace and head back to the Jesuit headquarters in Milltown, Dublin. At Milltown, they didn't know what to do with me. I had a bedroom and a room to use as an office, but I was something of an embarrassment. I had attracted the attention of the media and certain politicians, and since I was always identified as a Jesuit, I had drawn unwelcome attention to the Society. Apart from a few of the older men, closer to my generation, few people there seemed to have any grasp of or sympathy for what I had been doing. There was talk of the Society's commitment to Justice, but it was woolly, unfocused, and more theoretical than practical.

I was asked what I'd do next. I suggested, and was allocated the job of study and research into islands, and thus would be able to use my experience to help others. My answer was received almost gratefully, as if people were pleased I'd found something to do for myself. I think what I really needed was counselling, but none was forthcoming. I needed to experience that fraternity and fellowship for which the Society of Jesus had been founded in the first place, the fraternity based on the shared experience of Jesus Christ in the Spiritual Exercises. Instead, it took me the best part of two years to recover from Bishop Hegarty's decision, and I spent a great deal of that time simply sitting on the edge of my bed. Those were probably the two darkest years of my life, two years of acute mental agony.

Nor were those years devoid of irony. My arthritic hip deteriorated to such an extent that during the first few months back at Milltown I was eventually left with no option but to seek medical treatment. That in turn resulted in a hip replacement operation. I'd always refused to give into it on the island, I simply disguised my limp as best I could. If Bishop Hegarty had waited just six months longer, I would have been compelled to leave Tory on medical grounds.

Bishop Hegarty is no longer Bishop of Raphoe. At the time of writing, he is Bishop of Derry.

13

EPILOGUE

In Milltown Park, and not for the first time, the word 'perspective' became an important one in my life. Painfully and slowly, it began to dawn on me that being expelled from Tory, when viewed in the greater scheme of things, perhaps wasn't the worst thing that could have happened.

Time and time again I went back to that invaluable checklist of behaviour, the Discernment of Spirits, paid heed to the great Ignatian injunction to 'find God in all things' and started to apply some common sense to the situation. Maybe the Lord intended me to leave Tory Island. There were disadvantages to being island-bound; it made it that much harder to function on a broader canvas. A fair bit of the campaigning I'd done had taken place on the mainland; now that I was permanently back on the mainland – and in the capital – might I not be better able to operate on behalf of *all* the inhabited offshore islands? I hadn't been *banned* from Tory, I could visit it whenever I wanted to, and I'd now have greater access and mobility when it came to visiting other islands.

It was when I was on Tory that I thought of others in similar situations. When the weather began to turn – a rising, wild wind, a tempest of terrifying fury assailing the cliffs and rocks with unimaginable power and battering energy, the fog closing in to give the landscape such a chilling, eerie aspect, the squalls of scourging rain – I often thought of the other inhabited islands around the Irish coastline all suffering as we were. There had always been precious little talk of island development, and what there had been was hollow and hypocritical. It seemed that only economic criteria were employed (and even then in a flawed manner) whenever the future of the islands was considered. Island communities up and down the western seaboard were firmly anchored in the depression and rejection which ensue from deliberate neglect.

I began to form plans to develop an organization whose sole purpose was to work for and on behalf of *all* Ireland's offshore islands, and thus save the islanders' culture and heritage – what eventually became known as the All Ireland Islands Authority. Such a body could work towards the relief of poverty on the islands, advancing education and medical care, good transportation and communications, as well as fighting for the islanders' recognition by the government as part of the country's heritage. I started to canvas opinions and mobilize support among and from islanders. After a long, hard slog, I finally organized a special meeting in Cape Clear (on Clear Island, off the south-west coast of County Cork) in September 1984. A total of 50 people from places such as Inismaan, Iniseer, Tory, Sherkin, Bear Island and Rathlin attended.

Among the interested individuals was Fr (Dr) Eugene McDermott, a 75-year-old Doctor of Divinity, and a past curate on Aran Island, off County Donegal. He, too, had faced similar opposition and obstacles to his work. In the early '70s, in the columns of a national newspaper, he'd put the argument forward for optional celibacy for the Catholic clergy. He was immediately denounced for raising the subject – 'scandalous imprudence' – and attempts were made to shunt him off Aran Island. But he wouldn't move. He stayed put. He loved the islanders, cherished them as a community and feared for their future. The result? He stayed on for a further 11 years.

He wrote to me at the beginning of 1984, congratulating me on my work and wishing me well in my 'rescue' of Tory. 'You are certainly opening new avenues that should help to stabilize all the islands,' he wrote. 'Your work and courage for Tory helps all the islands and all neglected peoples. It is sad to see a community which was built up by the work of centuries fall apart. You are stopping it.' When I eventually met him (by then he had been moved to the parish of Termon) he reiterated his support for me and the campaign. 'You know, Diarmuid,' he said, 'maybe you should have stuck it out, the way I did. I just refused point blank to move. There was a whiff of bell, book and candle in the air. Maybe you should have refused to leave.'

His regard for and advocacy of island life were constantly strong and vibrant in him. I was delighted that he accepted the invitation to join the rest of us at Cape Clear. Like everyone else, I sat enthralled, saddened and inspired as he made an impassioned speech about the dangers to island communities caused by official indifference and neglect. He knew what he was talking about, he spoke from experience. Though he had returned from Aran Island three years previously, he still felt called to the island. When he took his pipe out of the right-hand side of his mouth, where it was clenched between his teeth, and talked passionately about the islands off Dungloe (south of Tory) that had been deserted 30 years ago, we hung on his every word.

'Inishal, Inishfree, Iniskeeragh, Rutland, Iniscoo, Iochtar, Idirnish, Owey – it's a sorrowful litany,' he said, 'and it mustn't happen again.'

When Tom Cecil from Rathlin Island said that they'd been inspired by our fight on Tory Island, and had taken on the challenge of officialdom, I knew I'd backed a winner in trying to set up this authority. But there was a long, bumpy road ahead.

In 1987, I made contact with the only person ever to have won both the Nobel and Lenin peace prizes. He was a former Irish government minister, chairman of Amnesty International, and United Nations commissioner for Namibia – Sean MacBride SC. I asked him if he could spare some time to see me at his home in Dublin, and he immediately agreed.

A charismatic man, the son of the famous Maud Gonne who had been the inspiration of W. B. Yeats' love poems, MacBride was bent over and frail-bodied when I met him. Within a year he would be dead. But on that day he was fully alert and listened keenly when I told him why I'd wanted to see him – to talk to him about the Island Trust. I explained in more detail the work that I hoped the organization would do. He listened intently and nodded as I spoke.

'What do you want me to do?' he asked.

'Would you become a trustee?' I replied. 'Can we use your name?'

'Certainly. Bring whatever papers you require me to sign, and I shall be delighted to sign them.'

Not only did he become a trustee and lend his name to our cause, he espoused it in the most energetic and wholehearted way – attending meetings, writing letters, making phone calls and lobbying. He harnessed all his energies and was an inspiration. In him, too, I'd backed a winner.

Nearly ten years on, we're still here, still fighting, proud that because of the sweat and tears and heartache we expended, the annoyance we caused, the publicity we created and the fight we put up, no other island off the Irish coastline has been evacuated.

And what of Tory? Well, it now has a £1 million hotel. Over £4 million has at last been allocated for the building of a conventional harbour for the island. I'm told it will cost about twice as much as the cost of a 'rock box' harbour. But it's EC money! It is late in the day, but better late ... There is also now a daily ferry service between Bunbeg on the mainland and Tory. But the airstrip is still on permanent hold.

I still keep in touch with my friends on Tory and have made several visits since the day I officially left. Two of my stalwart helpers, Pádraig Mac Rúairí and Shane Rogers, passed away within a short time of my leaving. I remain convinced that the exhaustion and stress which took their toll on all of us hastened Pádraig's death, and contributed massively to the stroke which eventually killed Shane. Jimmy Duggan – good, loyal and gifted – and his wife, Gráinne, are still on the island, and still imbued with the old spirit. Feilimidh Doohan is still alive and well. Mary Colgan, who was thrust into the roles of musical motivator and drama director, is still teaching but on the mainland, not far from Gweedore. She and her islander husband, Eddie Tom Doohan, visit the island occasionally. Mary McGinley, my housekeeper, also married an islander and has started a family. The fishermen are still fishing, the painters are still painting, and I still periodically take an Islands Art Exhibition around Ireland. The incumbent priest has now been on the island for 13 years; in the light of this, the bishop's comment that it was now common practice to move priests more frequently than usual seems somewhat shallow. I now work from Dublin, from a small, crowded basement office in Milltown Park. It has one barred window, backs on to a men's lavatory, and is nicknamed 'the bunker'. As for Bishop Hegarty, I haven't heard from him since 1984. The waves are still pounding against the rocks and cliffs of Tory, and the birds are still wheeling and swooping over the ocean. There are no lighthouse keepers any more – the lighthouse was automated in 1990 and demanned.

But the people of Tory are still speaking the purest Irish Gaelic to be heard anywhere in the world.

As I think of my work on Tory, and the difficulties I so often faced, the words of Decree 11 (from our 34th General Congregation in Rome) are particularly apt:

> ... *through their very apostolic responsibility, Jesuits are inevitably dragged into conflictual, even explosive situations. Our response to such situations can give rise to tensions with some Church authorities. Despite – indeed, because of – our sincere desire to live in fidelity to the Magisterium and the hierarchy, there may be times when we feel justified, even obliged, to speak out in a way that may not always win us general approval ... Ignatian obedience, in accord with the tradition of Catholic theology, has always recognized that our first fidelity must be to God, to the truth, and to a well-formed conscience. Obedience, then, cannot exclude our prayerful discernment of the course of action to be followed, one that may in some circumstances differ from the one suggested by our religious and Church superiors.*

I would like to think I followed these words in my actions over the years. In my own, small way, I wanted to emulate them through my campaign for a threatened community's rights to preserve its cultural integrity, and to control its own destiny and resources. The promotion of justice means working where people are now, not where we think they ought to be.

The debate on island development still continues. In March 1996 a report on this theme was debated in *Dáil Éireann*. The comments by various politicians reproduced here (taken from *Tuarisic Oifigiúil*, the Hansard equivalent) simply repeat what the Tory islanders and myself have been saying since 1981, and what we at the Island Trust now maintain.

The ongoing difficulties faced by the communities living on our offshore islands have been widely acknowledged. The need for a coherent Government response to this section of Irish society has led to the recent publication of the report of the Interdepartmental Co-ordinating Committee on Island development ... [the report] highlights a cycle of decline whereby out-migration as a result of the lack of economic opportunity and a reduced level of services combines with an ageing population to further undermine the sustainability of island life. This cycle of decline could ultimately lead to the desertion of many more islands and this would represent a major tragedy for the entire people of Ireland. Ireland's offshore islands are a linguistic, cultural and heritage asset to the nation and have a special inheritance and way of life which is unique ... The Government has also recognized the need for a partnership between island communities and State agencies which would allow islanders to be prime movers in strategies affecting their own future. Without question, the single most important issue facing island communities is access. The limited economic development of the island can be ascribed to factors such as access costs, poor infrastructure ... and peripherality. Many island communities have therefore been marginalized.

Donal Carey TD, Minister of State

When the Interdepartmental Committee sat around a table with a representative from every department, its prime objective was to ensure that no department lost control of any of its functions. That is the nature of civil servants participating in an interdepartmental committee but the function of the politicians should have been to ensure that the islanders' requirements were put ahead of departmental empire building. The islanders are ordinary Irish citizens. All they are seeking ... is that they be treated the same as everybody else, that they have the same right of access to services and to subsidies enjoyed by those in the cities, that they have the same right to education as people living on the mainland, that they have the same right to medical services and the same right to the standard of living enjoyed by people on the mainland.

Eamon Ó Cuív TD

I regret many councils aided and abetted people to leave the islands.

Mary Coughlan TD, niece of Deputy Clem Coughlan
(former Chairman of Donegal County Council)

During the Famine, one million people died while another one million emigrated. The depopulation of islands is on a par with that catastrophe ... [It] is a terrible indictment of us all, regardless of our political persuasion ... Ten or fifteen years ago, the island population [of Tory] was at the point of extinction. Donegal County Council had decided to build houses on the mainland for the people of the island, but ... the decline was halted.

Dinny McGinley TD

Their words sum up my story. Thanks to our work, Tory Island is still inhabited. We continue to campaign actively for better facilities, investment and development in the island. I shall continue to fight for the rights of the islanders until I drop.

If you would like to find out more about the Island Trust, please write to the following address:

Island Trust (Ireland)
Milltown Park
Dublin 6
Ireland
Telephone: (01) 2698411
Fax: (01) 2600371

THE SOUL OF POLITICS

A Practical and Prophetic Vision for Change

JIM WALLIS

With his first book in several years, Jim Wallis reinforces his reputation as one of the most powerful Christian voices of the modern era, a voice raised once more against the oppression of the weak by the powerful.

The Soul of Politics responds specifically to the signs of cultural breakdown and political impasse in Western societies: the absence of community, the widespread poverty, the violence, racism and sexism.

Wallis shows why both left and right wing visions are inadequate to the challenge of these problems. One preaches social justice, the other personal responsibility. The new political morality has to combine both, with a strong measure of spirituality too.

As the acquisitive eighties are left behind and we bask in the idea of the more 'caring' nineties, Jim Wallis's book is both a sharp reminder of cold reality and an encouraging manifesto for change.

'*What a thrilling, exhilarating experience reading* The Soul of Politics. *It is riveting stuff, just what the doctor ordered for a hardened, cynical and disheartened and disillusioned world ... This book shows how it is possible for all of us to become more human, living in an environment that is hospitable to people, where they matter, where justice and compassion and caring are at a premium. A tremendous and timely book.*'

Archbishop Desmond Tutu

DEAD MAN WALKING

HELEN PREJEAN

When Helen Prejean is invited to write to a prisoner on Death Row who brutally killed two teenagers, she has little idea how much it will change her life. Although she abhors his crime, she befriends one man as he faces the electric chair.

Dead Man Walking is Helen Prejean's gripping true story, which was nominated for the Pulitzer Prize. As powerful an indictment of the death penalty as has ever been written, it was recently made into an award-winning film directed by Tim Robbins, and starring Susan Sarandon and Sean Penn.

'*An extraordinary, compelling account of involvement with death row prisoners.*'

The Independent

'*Susan Sarandon gives the finest performance of her career.*'

Cosmopolitan

'*The most moving memoir of relationships with condemned men since Capote's "In Cold Blood".*'

The New Yorker

'*An intimate chamber piece for two, superbly acted. "Walking" is strong in every department.*'

Variety

CELTIC LIGHT

A Tradition Rediscovered

ESTHER DE WAAL

Celtic Christianity was forged with fire and light. It touches the heart as much as the mind. Here is an approach to the Christian life and faith which is vivid, vigorous, and totally down to earth.

This book, which is a reissue of *A World Made Whole*, presents a picture of a tradition in which light and dark, cross and creation, body and soul, time and eternity, inner and outer, east and west are all held together in creative unity. It is a fascinating introduction to Celtic spirituality.

In its pages we meet not only the great early saints such as St Patrick and St Columba, but the humble, anonymous people who still prayed with the traditional songs and blessings at home and in their work at the end of the last century.

'There is truth and beauty in this book.'

The Tablet

'A very engaging book … meticulously referenced with much fascinating historical information in a highly readable style.'

Church Times

THE JESUIT MYSTIQUE

DOUGLAS LETSON AND MICHAEL HIGGINS

The Society of Jesus, members of which are known as the Jesuits, was founded by St Ignatius of Loyola in 1540. It remains to this day one of the largest, most widespread and influential religious orders within the Roman Catholic Church. Since its inception, however, the Society of Jesus has attracted as much ill-informed speculation and rank prejudice as praise, based on the suspicion that it is a 'Church within a Church'.

This significant book puts the record straight. It looks at the contribution of modern Jesuits to education, liberation theology, literature, academic life and spirituality. It is based on an enormous number of interviews with members and former members the world over. They include Daniel Berrigan, Michael Campbell-Johnson, Michael Gallagher, the late Peter Hebblethwaite, Peter Levi, Jon Sobrino and Michael Walsh.

'This is a book to end all books on the Jesuit mystique. Almost everything good that can be said about the Society in the late twentieth century is said here.'

Thomas Clancy SJ, *National Jesuit News*

'Well written and well conceived...'

Lord Rawlinson, *Catholic Herald*